THE BUSINESS LETTER HANDBOOK

How to Write Effective Letters & Memos for Every Business Situation

Michael Muckian
& John Woods

Adams Media Corporation
HOLBROOK, MASSACHUSETTS

Published by Adams Media Corporation
260 Center Street, Holbrook, MA 02343

ISBN: 1-55850-614-4

Printed in Canada

J I H G F

Library of Congress Cataloging-in-Publication Data
Muckian, Michael.
The business letter handbook : how to write effective letters & memos for every
business situation / Michael Muckian & John Woods.
p.   cm.
ISBN 1-55850-614-4 (pb)
1. Commercial correspondence—Handbooks, manuals, etc. I. Woods, John A. II. Title.
HF5726.M87   1996
808'.066651—dc20   96-13660
CIP

This publication is designed to provide accurate and authoritative information with regard to the subject matter covered. It is sold with the understanding that the publisher is not engaged in rendering legal, accounting, or other professional advice. If legal advice or other expert assistance is required, the services of a competent professional person should be sought.
— From a *Declaration of Principles* jointly adopted by a Committee of the American Bar Association
and a Committee of Publishers and Associations

This book is available at quantity discounts for bulk purchases.
For information, call 1-800-872-5627
(in Massachusetts, 781-767-8100).

Visit our home page at: www.adamsmedia.com
Visit our exciting small business website at: www.businesstown.com

Contents

Acknowledgments

We'd like to acknowledge Dick Staron, our editor at
Adams Media Corporation, for suggesting this book
and for his support throughout its development.

Preface

This book has two purposes: (1) to introduce you to some basic ideas about successful written communication via letters and memos and (2) to give you about three hundred sample letters dealing with fifty-four different business situations that you can adapt for your own use.

Clear and effective writing reflects clear and effective thinking. Such writing facilitates business action. It eliminates confusion. It helps people understand the whats, whys, and hows of business policies and decisions. It cements relationships or diplomatically ends them. Poorly written letters and memos, conversely, make matters worse and reflect negatively on the writer.

Nearly all business action involves communication. Many of the problems that occur in any business can be traced to misunderstandings and unclear communication between people. Effectively written letters and memos help minimize such misunderstandings. By following the suggestions in the introduction to this book and using the sample letters as guidelines, you can more easily prepare written communications that will say what you want them to in a straightforward, friendly, businesslike manner.

To use this book in any communication situation in which you find yourself, simply check the letters in each category to find the one that best fits your needs and make changes as appropriate. It is possible and even probable that you will encounter various business problems that are not included in the list of situations the sample letters cover. That does not preclude using the samples anyway. Simply choose a situation similar to one in which you have an interest and adapt the letter to your purpose.

Many companies, regardless of size, have installed electronic mail systems to facilitate internal communication. Recognizing the growing popularity of this medium, we have also included a short section on the use of e-mail and a variety of sample messages showing the uses of e-mail and the composition of e-mail messages.

Finally, here are a few important notes on using the sample letters:

- All names, places, and situations in the sample letters are fictional—and any resemblance to real people, organizations, or events is coincidental.
- The sample letters offer good models to be followed—but in order to create your own clear and effective communications, they must be thoroughly adapted and changed to fit your situation.
- In cases where your communications involve legal issues or other professional or expert advice, be sure to also consult with a lawyer or other professional.

Introduction

You and Successful Written Communication

Countless hours have been spent defining what good communication is and, more importantly, how to do it. Theorists and social scientists draft diagrams of communications processes and develop complex social archetypes, all for the purpose of better understanding how people conceive and share ideas.

For our sake, however, let's dispense with ornate social theories. Plainly put, we either send or receive information via a common, mutually understood method. We then act on that information in some way.

Simpler still? You talk, write, or sign in a way you expect me to understand. I respond accordingly, using the same or a similar medium to signal my understanding, agreement, opposition, or any of dozens of other socially acceptable (or unacceptable) responses.

And no matter what the level of sophistication, all communications have one thing in common: They involve someone transmitting information and someone receiving. Eliminate either party and communication ceases to exist.

LETTERS AND COMMUNICATION

Business letters are no different. They're designed to inform, persuade, coerce, threaten, or just tell the recipient that his or her bill is past due. But if they're not written in a way that is easily understood and designed to effectively accomplish their goal, then they have not communicated and the task they are supposed to accomplish often goes undone.

Communication may be a two-way street, but the letter is a one-way medium. Unlike in conversation, there is no opportunity to seek clarification or refute major points during the course of the letter. To do so requires a return letter, which means more time, effort, and expense.

Any failure to communicate rests on you, the letter writer. True, some gaps simply cannot be bridged. But most can, and a good letter writer takes the responsibility for making the best effort possible to create such bridges, thus shortening the communication process and increasing the productivity in accomplishing the tasks the letter was sent out to promote.

Clarity and brevity in communication, especially in today's stimulus-choked society, is just common sense. But it is also part of an effort to enhance quality in the broader sense. No matter what your business philosophy, you know that professionalism leads to higher-quality operations and more effective results. And the more quality you can bring to your letters in terms of clarity, content, style, expediency, and completeness, the more time you save the recipient. Not only will that person appreciate understanding even bad news with a minimum amount of rhetorical gobbledygook, but you will accomplish your goal that much more quickly.

And from anyone's standpoint, that's good business.

THE ELEMENTS OF GOOD WRITING

Legend has it that Ernest Hemingway was a first-rate letter writer, turning to correspondence when his literary muse was trussed up in a corner, unable to inspire or perhaps not yet sober from the previous evening's revelry. He would write to friends, family, editors, and sometimes total strangers, sharing ideas, advice, insight, and information with much the same stylistic acuteness that earned him critical acclaim for novels like *The Sun Also Rises* and *A Farewell to Arms*.

Letter writing may be the only thing most of us have in common with Papa Hemingway. Although Hemingway had a distinct and recognizable style that is still parodied in literary competitions, much of his genius lay in his simple prose and, more importantly, clear expression of the thought and feeling behind the drama. He was an author who was clear in both thought and expression and whose meaning was seldom hard to discern. Maybe all that letter writing had something to do with it.

Some of us may try, but few can hope to be the next Hemingway. However, we can embrace some of the skills the author brought to his prose, as well as the notion that good writing often is invisible.

Too often business letters—or reports or memos or news releases or anything produced by people who get paid to sit behind a desk all day and push paper—fail to communicate for no other reason than that the authors mistake verbiage for communication and syllables for strength.

Packing letters with long words and phrases is a little like inviting eight of your best friends to play tennis on your side: Too much verbiage, like too many players, clutters up the court and impedes the play.

In most writing, less is generally more, provided that the words, thoughts, and phrases we use are simple, clear, and to the point. The best writers are the ones who can turn complex concepts into simple, clear prose, who can accomplish their mission in a sentence rather than a paragraph, and who know that words are only the medium, not the message.

Good writing often is an invisible framework for the concepts it promotes, and it does not draw attention to itself. Too much business writing consists of confusing phraseology, clichés, technobabble, and insufficiently drawn conclusions that fail to move the recipient to action.

These are not hurdles easily overcome. But overcoming them is a worthy goal, and an essential one for those who want to improve their communication ability and the value and impact of their written work.

SEVEN CS OF EFFECTIVE WRITING

Few things aid memory retention like a catchy phrase or a play on words. It makes something easier to remember and understand. Good writing has this type of educational tool at its disposal, and it can help us eliminate stiff, formal BusinessSpeak and replace it with a style that is more comfortable, and thus more effective.

One particular educational tool is called the *Seven Cs of Effective Writing*, and it describes effective prose as being:

1. *Clear.* This is the cornerstone of effective communication and requires considerable effort on the writer's part. It includes writing to the reader's level of understanding, but not down to the

The Seven Cs of Effective Writing

Clear

Complete

Concise

Concrete

Constructive

Conversational

Correct

reader. It means using language, words, and phrases that the reader understands, while avoiding all jargon and unfamiliar words and phrases. It involves coherently and logically ordering thoughts and ideas and structuring paragraphs so that each idea has its own place in the letter. Good narratives are designed to make the desired impact. Remember, it is the writer's obligation to clearly communicate so that the reader can understand, not the other way around.

2. *Complete.* Good writing includes all the information necessary to make the point and promote whatever action the letter requests. The data must be designed with a purpose in mind. Random details and thoughts, however colorful and interesting, only confuse the reader if they are not relevant to the issues being raised. Stay on track and make sure you have provided the reader with enough information to encourage the action you seek.

3. *Concise.* "Brevity is the soul of wit," William Shakespeare once wrote. Plainly put, keep letters short and to the point. Do not pad your communication if the padding does not address the main point or contribute to the letter's goal. Readers will be annoyed, not impressed, by verbiage that obstructs rather than expedites the communication process.

4. *Concrete.* Use numbers, ratios, and facts whenever they are available rather than prose that attempts to paraphrase those particulars. If you are talking about a recent order that has failed to arrive, identify the shipping code and contents of that order. This will help speed the process and clarify the communication's intent.

5. *Constructive.* Words and phrases that set a positive tone or cast recipients' actions (or inactions) in the most positive light possible receive a better response, and thus more effectively accomplish their goal. By giving the benefit of the doubt, you are more likely to get the reader on your side. It doesn't always work, but it's worth the effort.

6. *Conversational.* The bane of business communication tends to be the

BusinessSpeak in which much of it is written. Writing that is informal and conversational will be more easily understood and better received. You cannot afford to bypass the letter's other obligations and restrictions, but writing in a casual style will result in more effective communications.

7. **Correct.** Despite mastery of these other steps, letter writers cannot be effective if they ignore accuracy. This includes errors in structure, spelling, grammar, fact, and opinion. Make use of whatever spelling and grammar checking tools your word processor may have, and proofread drafts and finished copies rigorously. When possible, have another person proofread your letters. We all make mistakes, but even a tiny one creeping into your final text undermines your credibility as a communicator and casts a shadow over every other element of your message.

Is there a flip side to all of this? Are there Seven Deadly Sins of Writing? Just turn the Seven Cs around and you'll have those sins.

COMMUNICATING WITH PURPOSE

Letters are not the easiest way to communicate, nor are they the least expensive. When you take into consideration the time it takes to compose the letter, have it typed, check it for accuracy, have inaccuracies corrected, and have the letter mailed or faxed—well, why didn't you just pick up the telephone instead?

Letters often are necessary, however, for a variety of reasons we will cover a little later. More importantly, they enable an effective communicator to create a medium that goes beyond the surface purposes of informing and persuading into a deeper realm of political sensitivities. Some of those sensitivities are unique to individuals, firms, or situations; others are universal to the human race.

Volumes have been written on the psychology of communications. This is too lengthy and potentially boring to discuss here, but if there is a lesson to it all, it is that there are politics in language. You should choose words carefully to achieve the purpose of communication without antagonizing or offending the recipient in ways unintended by the letter writer.

Some areas of sensitivity are quite obvious. You must avoid comments that are racist, sexist, or demeaning. Other sensitive areas to avoid include actual political or social opinions that may offend your reader.

There are other elements of language that speak to the position of the recipient, the nature of the subject, or the goal of the letter writer that are more subtle. Awareness of these contributes to effective letter writing. We will note these elements as we use them in the various sample letters.

HOW TO WRITE A LETTER

Writing any kind of letter—and certainly an effective letter—requires basic understanding of several key communication components:

1. **Length and purpose.** The rule of thumb in length—provided you can include all the necessary components—is, the shorter the better. State your purpose, provide supporting information, and ask for whatever it is you are trying to accomplish. That is true whether you are trying to collect an overdue bill, inviting a corporate bigwig to speak at your next soirée, or commiserating with an employee over the death of a relative.

Different letters have different components, and thus are of different lengths. Knowing the purpose of your letter will help you decide how long that letter should be. The purpose is the guiding factor for things like content, tone, and structure.

2. *Format and structure.* Speaking of structure, there are different types of formats involving paragraph indenting and headings that you may want to experiment with. However, if your firm is an established one and therefore has been writing letters for years, chances are there already is a standard format. As long as that format is neat, simple, and consistently used, it will be serviceable for any type of letter you need to write.

Structure of the content, however, is a little different. While all letters vary based on purpose, audience, and writer, there are certain basic elements to be included:

A. The *return address* should be preprinted on the letterhead and should include complete company contact information, including telephone number and fax number (if there is one). If the company is large enough and the letter writer important enough, that person's name and title also may be preprinted on the letterhead. For example:

Marler Information Network
3131 Longwood Ave., P.O. Box 461
Kelso, Washington 97987
(800) 555-4647

James Marler
President/CEO

B. In the *addressee's information* the date may be flush left (known as block style), or it may be started at the center (modified block style) and balanced by the signature line at the bottom of the letter, also starting at the center. Here is an example of the more formal block style:

October 28, 1994

Ms. Tabatha Mead
Account Representative
Sky Chief Productions
31 Dogwood Ct.
Corvallis, OR 97876

In modified block style, you'll move the date line so it starts at the middle of the page.

C. The *salutation* usually begins with the standard "Dear . . . : " although other forms, such as including the recipient's name in the first line of the letter, have been known to creep in for more informal correspondence:

Dear Ms. Mead:

or

It has come to our attention,
Tabatha, . . .

D. The *body of the letter* should consist of an introductory paragraph that states the letter's purpose, supporting paragraphs that provide further information, and a closing paragraph that calls for action. Sentences are separated by one space, paragraphs by an extra line. The correct format also calls for "ragged right" rather than full right justification:

It has been several weeks since our last correspondence, and we have made great strides in developing our new computerized accounts network. Unfortunately, our working relationship has not. We have been expecting the down payment of $5,000 as indicated in our contract, and we cannot go ahead until your check arrives.

The contract, written April 13, specifies your order for receivers and cabling to connect to our interactive data network. Based on that order, we have purchased supplies and subcontracted for additional services to meet your needs. Our crew is eager to begin its work, but we need your deposit in hand before we can get the process underway.

We remember your enthusiasm during our discussion, and we wonder what problem may have arisen that has delayed your down payment. If there is anything we can do to help, please feel free to call. Otherwise, we will anticipate receiving payment within 10 days.

Thank you for your kind attention to this matter, Tabatha. We look forward to working with you.

E. The *closing* and *signature line*, also standard, should be placed flush left in block style or start at the middle of the page to balance the date line in modified block style. The sentiments depend on the writer's sensitivities and the situation.

    Sincerely,

    Signature

    James Marler
    President/CEO

F. *Reference information* follows the signature and usually includes capitalized initials of the letter's composer and lowercase initials of the typist or word processor, separated by a slash. Enclosures are indicated below the initials, as are the recipients of duplicate copies of the letter.

JM/bg
Enclosure
CC: Fred Robideaux, Robideaux and Smythe, Attorneys at Law

There also are variations on block and modified block style. How closely your letters are tied to traditional format will depend on your firm, its policies, the nature of your letter, the nature of your relationship with the recipient, and a host of content-related issues. Your best bet is to create a style or standard and stick to it for all written communications. Like your name or your logo, your style becomes part of your image. Inconsistencies in that style can send the recipient a negative message about you or your firm. Figures 1 and 2 illustrate and explain the block and modified block styles.

LETTERHEAD

-
-
-
-
-

Date

→

Addressee's Name
Company Name
Street Address or PO Box No.
City, ST ZIP

→

Salutation:

→

This letter-style example is presented using block style.

→

In the block style, every letter part used begins at the left margin. This feature makes the block-style letter one of the easiest and quickest to produce.

→

You will generally prepare business letters in block style on letterhead stationery. The dateline begins the letter. Present paragraphs in a single-spaced format. A double space separates the paragraphs. The letter is left-justified with uneven line lengths, which is the appropriate style for all letters.

→

Because of its easy-to-produce features, the block style is among the most widely used letter styles.

→

Complimentary close,

→

Signature

→

Sender's Typed Name
Sender's Title

→

Reference Information

● = Variable spacing depending on letter length
→ = One blank line

Figure 1. Block-style letter

LETTERHEAD

●
●

Date

→

Addressee's Name
Company Name
Street Address or PO Box No.
City, ST ZIP
→

Salutation:
→

This letter is presented using modified block style. The paragraphs explain some differences from the block style.
→

Letters using modified block style begin the return address and the dateline at the horizontal center of the page. The complimentary close, sender's typed name, sender's signature, and sender's official title also begin at the horizontal center of the page. Vertical spacing is the same as for the block style.
→

In using the modified block style, the writer can choose either to indent the paragraphs or to use blocked paragraphs. This example shows the use of indented paragraphs. The letter is left-justified with uneven line lengths, which is the appropriate style for all letters.
→

Many letter writers choose the modified block style because of its more balanced appearance. However, beginning as many as four lines at the center and indenting paragraphs does take a little more time. You can set this style up using your word processor, eliminating these formatting problems.
→

Complimentary close,

→

Signature

→

Sender's Typed Name
Sender's Title

→

Reference Information

● = Variable spacing depending on letter length
→ = One blank line

Figure 2. Modified block letter

The line down the middle shows the proper placement of date and closing.

G. When *addressing envelopes*, the U.S. Post Office recommends that the address be typed in all capital letters with no punctuation. This facilitates the operation of machines that can "read" addresses. For example:

MS TABATHA MEAD
SKY CHIEF PRODUCTIONS
31 DOGWOOD CT
CORVALLIS OR 97876

3. *Language and tone.* Language usage can be formal or informal, depending on your intent. Strive for clarity and proper word usage. Carefully avoid language misuse, impropriety, and crudeness. Letters have a way of turning up where you least expect them, and an off-color comment, no matter how appropriate it may have been for the recipient, can come back to haunt you.

   Likewise, the tone should be at least neutral and at best upbeat and positive. You gain little with letters that have a negative flavor, even when communicating unpleasant circumstances. You catch flies more easily with sugar than with vinegar, and that holds true for letters as well as for speech.

4. *Audience and intent.* Your tone, language, format, and even structure may be determined solely by the nature of your audience and the intent of the letter. You should write all letters to your audience's perceived level of education and sophistication, even if it means taking a guess. If your language is correct, your meaning clear, and your approach simple, you run less risk writing just a little above your readers than you do writing down to them. Avoid jargon and presumption and you should do fine.

WHEN AND WHY TO WRITE LETTERS

● **For the record.** Letters provide permanent records for businesses that need a paper trail to track contract dealings or a record of collection attempts, or that need to copy the correspondence for nonrecipients, or for files.

● **For clarity and common understanding.** Letters allow writers to clearly and completely express what's on their minds. Unlike verbal conversation, in which perceptions of the information shared are formed immediately, letters allow for greater clarity and inclusion of detail.

● **For reflection.** You can better communicate complex ideas or controversial thoughts in letter format because it allows for reflection, discussion, and reconsideration.

● **For action.** Because of their ability to be shared, letters can become a rallying point for recipients and a call to action for those concerned with the letters' content.

GETTING READY TO WRITE

Like most other activities, good writing takes preparation time as well as performance time. In fact, the better the preparation, the better the performance. That's not to say that a letter writer must spend hours considering the ramifications of his or her message, but some time must be spent doing the following prewriting activities:

● **Defining concepts.** What will your letter be about? To whom will it be directed? What purpose will it try to achieve? These are basic questions, but sometimes writers attempt to draft the text before gathering all the necessary information. That is when errors, omissions, inaccurate concepts, language misuse, and other problems begin creeping in. The tighter the definition of purpose you can generate in the prewriting phase, the more effective (and less time-consuming) the actual writing experience will be.

- **Choosing tools.** Will your ideas be communicated by formal letter or informal memo? Is electronic mail via computer network an option to consider? What about handwritten addendums to the letter, or even entirely handwritten notes in lieu of a letter? Answers to all these questions will depend on the communication's circumstances, recipient, occasion, and purpose. Determining this during the prewriting phase will make your final effort more effective.

- **Frame of reference/frame of mind.** Under what circumstances are you drafting this letter or memo? What role do you play in the communication's purpose? Is this a representation only of your firm (such as an overdue notice) or a personal communication from you as a representative of the firm (such as a personal plea to a fellow executive for a charitable contribution)? Knowing your frame of reference and frame of mind will help you keep from subconsciously undermining your communication.

  Some of the most deadly political crossfires have been started by written correpondence whose writer did not fully appreciate the business or psychological impact the letter might have on the reader. A second set of eyes reviewing for political context also can help you avoid such situations.

SOME WORDS OF CAUTION BEFORE YOU BEGIN

- **Letters are permanent**. Something said in the heat of a telephone call may easily be softened, if not forgotten altogether, as the issue is ironed out. Copies of letters, however, tend to hang around and tickle old wounds long after those wounds otherwise would have healed.

- **Letters are powerful.** In today's busy society, the mere fact that someone has taken the time to sit down and draft a letter rather than making a telephone call may indicate that the writer sees the issue as of greater importance. Couple that with corporate letterhead, and suddenly the impact has increased dramatically. Attorneys tend to write letters for a variety of reasons. Such an impact is one of those reasons.

- **Letters are evidence.** The role letters play as documentation in the nation's legal system is another reason why attorneys write them. They are proof that someone said and intended something. They are secondary proof that people have done what they said they would do. They effectively establish the paper trail that lawyers and judges so dearly cherish. The same holds true in corporate politics. In fact, many letters are written as much for the copies for fellow executives or some general information file that they provide as for the original correspondence value.

- **Letters reflect communication skills level—over and over again.** A poorly written letter will harm your credibility more than all but the most heinous public incidents. You may talk in "aw shucks" language, and people will perceive you as down-to-earth and friendly. But just try writing with the same level of grammatical shortcuts and casualness, and suddenly the response is very different.

  And, since letters often hang around and people may bring them out at the most inappropriate or embarrassing times, you may have the opportunity to disprove your ignorance—over and over and over.

THE IMPORTANCE OF LANGUAGE CLARITY

The bane of business communication is that often the message doesn't get through because it's not easily understood by the listener or reader. If communication is a two-way street, then BusinessSpeak, as we often see it, leads to a dead end.

The core of communication is clarity, and that characteristic is the one that is often the most difficult to achieve. Simple writing, like plain speaking, requires a great deal more effort than mere regurgitation of text. Many writers do not understand that, and rely instead on jargon, complexity, impersonal sentences, and words that are too long for their own good when writing letters, memos, and reports.

As a communicator, your goal is to share your thoughts, ideas, and directives with as much clarity, simplicity, and purpose as possible. The shorter your sentences—up to a point, at least—the better. The simpler your sentence structure, the clearer your message. The more forthright your tone, the greater your impact. It's that simple.

BUT IT ISN'T SIMPLE AT ALL

Communicators who find letter writing easy either spend hours out of each day doing it or are fooling themselves. Even bad writing is tough work, and good writing can be an excruciating experience for those who are unprepared. But there are a few simple tools that all of us have at our disposal that can make the process easier and more effective. Let's review them.

- **Write in the active rather than the passive voice.** State your purpose directly, with subject preceding verb, and the impact of what you say will be stronger and more to the point. For example:

  We expect payment of both the amount that we agreed on and the penalties indicated in clause 4b of the contract.

That is a much stronger statement than

  Payment is expected of the sum that was contracted by us and the penalties that were indicated in clause 4b.

Use the active voice to make your prose stronger and more direct.

- **Vary sentence length and structure to manage and direct your letter's impact.** Overlong sentences often are confusing, lack strong direction, and contain too many elements, all of which dull their impact. Short sentences are easy to understand. However, varying your sentence lengths works best. You may think that using only short sentences is the best way to write, but doing this can make your writing boring. For example, consider the following:

  We are planning a new training program. We will explore moving to total quality management. The training starts next Tuesday. You will receive study materials tomorrow. Please review them. Bring your materials to training. Be prepared with three questions.

Or:

  We are planning a new training program on total quality management. Our initial session begins next Tuesday. You will receive your study materials tomorrow. Please review them ahead of time, bring them with you, and be prepared with three questions.

While the first example is clear, it is also machine-gun-like in the way it reads—point, point, point—and it eliminates any personality from the writing. The second piece varies sentence length and is easier to read and remember.

- **Use modifiers to build the intensity of your impression**. If you remember way back to Mrs. O'Leary's grammar lessons, an adjective is a word that modifies a noun ("the *oak-lined* executive suite"), and an adverb is a word that modifies a verb ("she *rapidly* advanced to the executive level"). Too many business writers forget what Mrs. O'Leary taught all of us: Sentences and phrases have a greater impact when they paint more vivid word pictures. That means that a letter's clarity and communication value can be enhanced by the use of vivid, but appropriate, modifiers. ("She *puposefully* and *rapidly* advanced to the *large, rich-looking, oak-lined* executive suite.") However, also remember that too many adjectives and adverbs can be distracting, undermining your communication.
- **Master your verb power.** Verbs bring action to sentences, and the stronger the verb, the clearer the message. Consider:

  Mr. Frederickson was promoted to vice president last week. Please send your congratulations.

  Or:

  Mr. Frederickson earned his stripes, and we're pleased to announce his rise to the level of vice president. Help us applaud his accomplishment.

  All right, so we added a little color to that one. But the example further illustrates the ability to use multiple tools to create a more vivid impression.
- **Be familiar rather than formal.** Stiffness and overly formal approaches still plague all forms of business communication. Writers can be more effective if they lighten up, while still treating the situation with respect.

  The agreement between Forrestal Associates and Kelvin Industries indicates that each will be responsible for its own expenses in the upcoming series of research projects to contribute to greater operational efficiencies and more stringent accounting requirements.

  Or:

  As we agreed, Forrestal and Kelvin will each cover its own expenses. This promotes better cost management as well as making our accounting staff more confident in its operations.

- **The I/we issue.** England's Queen Victoria immortalized the regal presence with the statement, "We are not amused," presumably directed at some witticism uttered by Prime Minister Benjamin Disraeli. Since she was a portly woman, she may have been unconsciously referring to more than her regal authority.

  Needless to say, the use of "we" is less personal and considered more formal. In discussing the firm, it is more appropriate than "I," which is informal and distinctly personal. But "we" does distance the writer from the reader, putting the onus of corporate authority in between.

  Whenever possible, refer to your company in the abstract. (A company is an "it," not a "they.") Use "we" when necessary and in formal situations; use "I" when expressing your personal opinion, which is usually most appropriate when you know the recipient.
- **Color and detail.** We referred to this earlier in the adjective/adverb section.

The more specific you can make your letters, and the more detail you can include, the greater your letter's impact. But you must stay on track! Extraneous detail, like too much jewelry, distracts rather than enhances. But color and detail that are carefully chosen and strategically placed can strengthen your text and provide the information necessary for reaction and response.

- **The little matter of tone.** Different letters are written for different purposes, and thus require different tonal components. But keeping even bad news as positive as possible, or at least within the appropriate tonal requirements, can enhance a letter's communication effectiveness. Consider the much-abused job applicant rejection letter. Which would you prefer receiving?

> We had a wide range of candidates from which to choose, and we selected the person we felt had the most outstanding qualifications for the position. As you may surmise, that person was not you.

Or:

> Competition for this position was difficult, with many excellent candidates. Your credentials were quite impressive, but we regret to say that they did not quite match the needs of the position. We hope someday to have another position that is more consistent with your skills.

- **Tone contributes to whether you make a positive or a negative impression on your reader.** Have someone who understands either the recipient or the situation read your draft if at all possible. He or she may help you detect subconscious characteristics that may be sliding into your prose and turning it in a way you would rather it not go.

- **Know your paragraph basics.** Mrs. O'Leary also taught us that a paragraph should contain one main idea (a "topic sentence," she called it) accompanied by supporting documentation. You can construct the paragraphs in your letters in the same fashion, with one main idea followed (or preceded) by supporting points. This makes it easy for the reader to understand your point, as well as aiding in secondary references. ("In the third paragraph of your January 16 letter, you stated our project's mission and its ancillary goals.")

There are other, more subtle approaches, but these are the basic tools in any letter writer's toolbox. You will see them applied throughout the text, helping to customize basic approaches into stronger, more personal letters.

BASIC LETTER COMPONENTS—A REVIEW

We have now covered the major points, but it does not hurt to review the basics of good letter construction:

1. **Define your letter's purpose and audience.** From those two factors, you can better determine language, tone, length, intent, and structure.

2. **Identify the proper letter format.** In most cases, your corporate style will determine what that will be.

3. **Draft your letter using as many tools from your writer's toolbox as possible.** Letters may be memorable for all the right—or all the wrong—reasons. But they will be effective in helping you accomplish your goals only if they are done right.

4. **Let another interested party review the draft if possible.** Too often letters leave offices laden with errors, written in the wrong tone, aimed at the wrong group, or setting out to accomplish the

wrong goals only because the writer did not have the time or inclination to have the letter reviewed by a second set of eyes. Do not be too proud to have someone proofread and edit your work. All of the best writers are subject to strict editorial scrutiny. That is part of why they write as well as they do.

5. **Correct all errors, scrupulously check all facts, and make sure the final version is error-free.** Anything that is in any way questionable is better left unsaid. Remember the old newspaper editors' maxim: When in doubt, take it out. Once you have accomplished all that, your letter should be ready to send.

The Letters

What follows are approximately three hundred examples of letters and memos designed to help you craft your own more effective communications for a large number of different business and personal situations. We have grouped the letters by type in alphabetical order.

Throughout the text, you will find skeleton structures, designed to be filled with your own facts and data, for the more common types of letters. We believe that the mix of more creative approaches and structural outlines should give even the most casual letter writer both basic and advanced approaches and examples covering common problems.

Finally, the book concludes with pointers on the use of e-mail and various examples of e-mail messages.

1a. ACCOMPLISHMENTS—CORPORATE

Date

Name/Title
Business/Organization Name
Address
City, State ZIP

Dear Chairman (*name*):

We will release our annual report within the week, but I wanted to reach you first with our good news. Not only has the firm reached its projected budget increases of 6.3 percent in all categories, but several categories have surpassed their goals by as much as 3 percent. This means corporate performance has not only improved but, in light of the current financial climate facing our industry, exceeded our most optimistic expectations.

Specifically, overall revenues in all categories met or only slightly missed budgeted goals. The greatest disparity was less than 3 percent. In several categories—notably electronic applications, bulk distribution, and specialty services—performance exceeded budget by 1.3 percent to 4.9 percent. Our average overall revenue increase totaled 7.2 percent, or 0.9 percent more than budget.

Operational cost savings also exceeded expectations. If you will recall, we had projected cost reductions totaling 18 percent compared to last year's operational budget. While some categories varied, our overall reduction totaled 23 percent, or 5 percent more than the budgeted amount.

Chief Financial Officer Jeffrey Toole will brief the entire board on all details at this month's meeting. But I chose to exercise my right as chief executive officer to share the good news with you first. I know Jeff won't mind.

If you have any questions, please feel free to call either Jeff or me. Otherwise, we look forward to a productive board meeting and a prosperous new year.

Best regards,

Signature

Name
Title

1b. ACCOMPLISHMENTS—DEPARTMENTAL

MEMORANDUM

TO: All Departments
FROM: President
DATE:
SUBJECT: Outstanding Achievement

In today's competitive marketplace, innovation and originality are important. But unless they are accompanied by the ability to get to market first with new products and services, they do little to accomplish corporate goals. We are proud to recognize a department within our own firm that has mastered all three levels of achievement.

Molecular Development, which explores and analyzes the molecular structures that make up the compounds on which many of our products are based, has discovered new applications for a familiar compound that have reduced costs and production time. The department's efforts also set the stage for new product development that could revolutionize the cosmetics industry. This past week, the department received a new federal patent that will enable us to command a new segment of the market and set the stage for aggressive growth into the next century.

Our appreciation and thanks go to John Edelstein and his group of chemists and analysts. Under his leadership and through their teamwork, they have helped position our firm as an industry leader. We all owe them our congratulations and thanks.

1C. ACCOMPLISHMENTS—PERSONAL

Date

Name/Title
Business/Organization Name
Address
City, State ZIP

Dear (*name*):

The news of your appointment as vice president has yet to hit the street, and no doubt it will make more than one of your company's competitors nervous. But let me be the first to say

CONGRATULATIONS

on this outstanding achievement. Few deserve it more, and I know no one who could do the job better.

Before your schedule heats up, we'd like to take you and Alice out to dinner to help you celebrate the honor. You have been so supportive over the years that such a trifle hardly compensates, but Peg and I would be pleased if you two would find the time to join us and help us recognize the rise to the top of one of our own.

You know where to find us. We await your call. In the interim, again, heartiest congratulations.

Sincerely,

Signature

Name
Title

2a. ADJUSTMENTS—POSITIVE

Date

Name/Title
Business/Organization Name
Address
City, State ZIP

Dear (*name*):

You certainly drive a hard bargain. That was what Mr. Tempe said when I shared with him your complaint about the printing quality on the last press run of *The Legal Eagle*. The colors didn't register properly, you said. The lines in the descending letters often were broken, you noted. The overall job was smudged, you complained.

Mr. Tempe, who is responsible for quality control in the main printing shop, reviewed both the work and your assertions. He believes you are right. Because of a crew shortage, a press was misaligned and resulted in a compromise in our quality on this job. You will not be charged for the run.

In light of the fact that the magazines already have been mailed to subscribers and cannot be recalled or rerun, we also will deduct 15 percent from your next run of *The Legal Eagle* to help compensate you for the inconvenience to you and your readers caused by our mistake on the last issue. We realize this wasn't part of your make-good request, but we value your years of doing business with us, and want to continue to serve your printing needs in the future.

We regret that this happened and hope the actions we have taken make up for it. If there is anything else we can do, please don't hesitate to call.

Sincerely,

Signature

Name
Title

2b. ADJUSTMENTS—NEGATIVE

Date

Name/Title
Address
City, State ZIP

Dear (*name*):

Thank you for writing us about the malfunction of your microwave oven while preparing our popcorn. We're sorry the glass plate beneath the bag of corn shattered during the procedure. We sincerely hope no one was injured by the broken glass.

We note on the back panel of the box that microwave popping corn generates a great deal of heat at the point at which the bag comes in contact with the platform in the oven. This is due to the concentration of oil and seeds there. That is why the cautions on the back panel of the box and on the bag itself note that care should be taken and an unbreakable platform used when preparing this product.

Such damage happens occasionally, and we sometimes receive letters of complaint asking us for compensation or replacement of the parts damaged during the popping procedure. While we would like to accommodate such requests, we have no way of knowing whether the problems lie with our product or with not following directions or with a faulty oven. Without knowing more, we cannot take responsibility.

However, we have enclosed three coupons for complimentary boxes of our microwave popcorn. We appreciate your patronage.

With best wishes,

Signature

Name
Title

3a. ANNIVERSARY DATES—CORPORATE

Date

Name/Title
Business/Organization Name
Address
City, State ZIP

Dear (*name*):

No doubt the flags are flying and the champagne corks popping at your corporate headquarters. We'd like to join the happy crowd wishing you heartiest congratulations on your 25 years serving the automotive needs of American consumers.

As a major supplier to your firm for the past 15 years, we appreciate having had the opportunity to help position you as one of the preeminent manufacturers of automotive parts in the country. It has been a beneficial journey for both our firms, and we are glad to have been part of the excitement.

A toast to you on your 25th anniversary. Here's hoping the next 25 years will be even more successful for all of us.

Best regards,
Signature
Name
Title

3b. ANNIVERSARY DATES—PERSONNEL

MEMORANDUM

TO: Name
FROM:
DATE:
SUBJECT: Your Silver Anniversary

These days, employees who are totally committed to making their firm a success are like gold, Gene. Your past 25 years of hard work, contributions, and continue corporate advancement make you one of those rare people. We appreciate everything you have done for our company.

In reviewing past performance records, it is clear that your contributions have had a significant impact on our success. According to our policy, you will be receiving the usual accolades and public appreciation. But in this instance, I wanted to add my own personal note of thanks.

You have never swayed from your task, you have always supported your colleagues, and you have helped make our product the industry's leader. We'd have had a hard time doing it without you. And for that I am deeply indebted.

3C. ANNIVERSARY DATES—GENERIC

Date

Name/Title
Business/Organization Name
Address
City, State ZIP

Dear *(name)*:

It is our distinct pleasure to commend and recognize *(complete name of firm)* on its *(name of achievement or number of anniversary)*. Under your leadership, your firm's contributions to the industry have been many. Despite the challenges facing today's *(name of product)* providers, *(shortened name of firm)* has long been known for its outstanding performance and service.

(Optional paragraph 1: Outline recent corporate achievements, using two to three examples to draw a single conclusion of excellent performance or outstanding service.)

(Optional paragraph 2: Outline superior individual performance or corporate performance under the leadership of the letter's recipient. Follow the same approach used in Optional Paragraph 1.)

We recognize the continued challenges facing the *(name of industry)* industry. We have no doubt that *(name of firm)* will continue to excel in providing America's demanding consumers with excellence in both products and service.

Our hats are off to you. Best of luck carving new *(shortened name of industry)* industry frontiers in the future.

Sincerely,

Signature

Name
Title

4a. ANNOUNCEMENTS—GENERIC

Date

Name/Title
Business/Organization Name
Address
City, State ZIP

Dear (*name*):

Communication is important to any business, and we wanted you to be among the first to know that as of *(date of announcement's effectiveness)*, *(name of firm)* *(purpose of announcement)*.

(*Optional paragraph 1: Explain the rationale for the change, highlighting those characteristics affecting the letter recipient's company.*)

(*Optional paragraph 2: Explain how the change will better improve service to or the relationship with the letter recipient's company.*)

If you have any questions at all about *(description of change)*, feel free to contact me at *(address and/or telephone number)*. Your relationship with our firm is important, and we hope that this change will only enhance the work we have already begun together.

Very best regards,

Signature

Name
Title

4b. ANNOUNCEMENTS—MERGERS, ACQUISITIONS, AND TAKEOVERS

Date

Name/Title
Business/Organization Name
Address
City, State ZIP

Dear (*name*):

This letter serves as formal notice to you as chairman and to the rest of the board that the National Credit Union Administration has directed that the assets and members of Cloverleaf Federal Credit Union be merged with those of Deep Woods Federal Credit Union, effective November 1. You have been notified orally by administration representatives, and they will be following up with their own written notification shortly.

In the administration's eyes, this merger is necessary for the safety and protection of both credit union members' funds, and the industry's insurance fund. The board of Cloverleaf Federal Credit Union will be retained in an advisory capacity for six months beginning October 1 to help effect a smooth merger.

The administration recognizes and appreciates the assistance you and your fellow directors have provided in facilitating this merger, and holds none of you accountable for the tenuous financial condition into which Cloverleaf fell after the closing of its primary sponsor, Blacktop Industries.

As chairman of Deep Woods Federal Credit Union, I look forward to working with you to protect the assets of your members. We appreciate your contributions, both now and over the next few months, and know our merger efforts will be successful.

Sincerely,

Signature

Name
Title

4c: ANNOUNCEMENTS—PERSONNEL

MEMORANDUM

TO: All Departments
FROM: Vice President, Personnel
DATE:
SUBJECT: Karl Octet becomes SVP/Research

Karl Octet has been named senior vice president of research for American Oscilloscope. The appointment is effective April 15.

Prior to coming here, Mr. Octet was vice president of new product development at Terpsichore Industries, manufacturers of electronic radar components in conjunction with McDonnell-Douglas for use in jet fighter aircraft. Before that, Mr. Octet worked in product development at the Boeing Corporation.

Mr. Octet holds a bachelor's degree from Northwestern University, a master's degree in applied sciences from Stanford University, and a doctorate from Massachusetts Institute of Technology. His writings have been published extensively in both *The Radar Journal* and *Modern Corporate Technology*.

We will hold a reception this Friday to introduce Mr. Octet to all division and department heads. Please plan on joining us to help welcome Karl to American Oscilloscope.

4d. ANNOUNCEMENTS—NEW BUSINESS RELATIONSHIPS

MEMORANDUM

TO: Name/Title
FROM: Purchasing
DATE:
SUBJECT: Change in Suppliers

Don't look for Bob Strong from United Office Products to be around anymore. Bob called this morning to inform me that he has left UOP, and that the office products supplier has just filed for Chapter 11 bankruptcy protection from its creditors.

Bob is not implicated in the restructuring or debt collection proceedings and is looking for a similar position at another company. We may be doing business with him in the future, but effective immediately all office products requests will be handled through this department and Marvin Ving, sales manager for Desk Job, another office supplies company.

As always, we appreciate any input regarding past dealings—good or bad—anyone has had with either Mr. Ving or Desk Job. We hope this change will not interrupt service or inconvenience any department. All UOP backorders will be transferred to Marv immediately.

4e. ANNOUNCEMENTS—RELOCATION

Date

Name/Title
Business/Organization Name
Address
City, State ZIP

Dear (*name*):

Growth is often the byproduct of success. We are writing you to announce that because of our recent success, (as of September 1) we will be moving to a larger, more modern facility.

In addition to more than doubling our floor space, our new address in the recently refurbished Cropduster Building in the heart of downtown also provides us with modern communications facilities, easier delivery access, and much more storage space. We also believe our move back downtown shows our support for the community we're all part of.

We welcome your visit! Please drop by at our new address:

> Shenk, Hatfield & McCoy
> Cropduster Building, Ste. 600
> Cropduster Plaza
> Lima, Ohio 34267

We look forward to seeing you.

Best regards,

Signature

Name
Title

5a. ANNUAL MEETINGS—NOTICE OF MEETING

MEMORANDUM

TO: All Stockholders, Directors, and Staff
FROM: President's Office
DATE:
SUBJECT: Annual Meeting

The Eclipse Corporation's annual meeting and financial report will be held Friday, June 9, 1995 in the Festival Ballroom of the Hilton Hotel and Towers, Oklahoma City, Oklahoma, at 10 a.m. All stockholders, directors, staff, and interested parties are invited to attend.

The firm's financial condition will top the agenda, with a comprehensive report by Chief Financial Officer Marilyn Sobczyk. The accounting firm of Shaker, Peabody & Goode, Eclipse Corporation's independent auditing firm, also will present its analysis.

The company's human resources and marketing departments will offer brief insights into the challenges and opportunities facing their specific departments. The meeting will also include a presentation by the president and the election of new board members.

If you cannot attend, please plan to send a proxy for voting purposes. If authorized, a proxy will be appointed on your behalf from among the existing directors.

5b. Annual Meeting—Shareholders' Proxy Ballot

Date

Dear Shareholder:

The annual meeting of Eclipse Industries will be held in the Festival Ballroom at the Hilton Hotel and Towers, Oklahoma City, Oklahoma, June 9, 1995. The board of directors has called for a stockholder vote on several important amendments as outlined in the attached proxy statement.

Specifically, those amendments are as follows:

- Amendment 16 to Article 36: Reduction in employee health coverage and increase in employee copayments for such coverage.

- Amendment 41 to Article 9: Restratification of stockholder benefits to address increased operating expenses.

- Election of new board members.

If you are unable to attend, please indicate your intentions by completing the following:

___ I AUTHORIZE board members of Eclipse Industries to vote on my behalf.

___ I DO NOT AUTHORIZE board members of Eclipse Industries to vote on my behalf.

Signature_____

Printed Name_____

Proxy slips must be returned to Eclipse Industries headquarters no later than June 1. Please use the enclosed postage-paid envelope.

Thank you for your cooperation.

Sincerely,

Signature

Name
Title

6a. ANNUAL REPORTS—ACCOMPANYING LETTER

Date
Name/Title
Business/Organization Name
Address
City, State ZIP

Dear (*name*):

"Clear Vision for a Bright Future."

That was the theme that the Seacrest Optical Services board of directors chose for this year's strategic move into new markets and new technologies in eye care and eyewear. That is also the name of Seacrest's enclosed annual report, in which we have outlined the successful steps we have taken toward those twin goals. We are happy to send you a copy of that report.

You'll see that it outlines how Seacrest met both its financial and its service goals in an economic environment rife with challenges. The report also sets the stage for phase two of the aggressive growth effort, toward which we have already begun moving.

Thank you for your interest in Seacrest. We hope "Clear Vision for a Bright Future" answers your questions about Seacrest Optical Services operations, and shows you the direction in which we are headed. We would welcome your investment in our company.

Very truly yours,

Signature

Name
Title

6b. ANNUAL REPORT—POSITIVE RESPONSE

Date

Name/Title
Business/Organization Name
Address
City, State ZIP

Dear (*name*):

Some people think annual reports all look alike after a while. But "Clear Vision for a Bright Future" certainly brings the accomplishments of Seacrest Optical Services into focus. Congratulations on both an impressive report and an impressive year.

I look forward to my association with your company as a shareholder and consumer.

Sincerely,

Signature

Name
Title

6c. ANNUAL REPORT—NEGATIVE RESPONSE

Date
Name/Title
Business/Organization Name
Address
City, State ZIP

Dear (*name*):

As an investor in Seacrest Optical Services, I was less than thrilled by the company's weak financial performance last year. I understand that such things happen, particularly in light of the weak economy facing the entire nation. But I can neither understand nor condone the highly polished—and obviously expensive—annual report I just received from you.

These are times for belt-tightening, not promotional extravagance. I need the financial performance information, but attempting to hide the red ink behind slick photographs, glossy paper stock, and expensive publishing tricks and techniques is a poor way to spend investors' money. The firm is in enough trouble. How can you justify adding additional expense to existing injury?

I will be contacting my broker soon about moving some of my investments around. If I don't receive a satisfactory response from Seacrest President Morley Murphy within two weeks about this matter, I will consider selling my Seacrest stock.

I look forward to your forthcoming response.

Sincerely,

Signature

Name

7a. APOLOGIES—GENERIC

Date
Name/Title
Business/Organization Name
Address
City, State ZIP

Dear (*name*):

Thank you for bringing to our attention *(full identification of problem)*. Our firm normally prides itself on avoiding such situations. This is not part of the norm for us, and we are sincerely sorry for any inconveniences you may have suffered because of *(short definition of problem)*.

*(**Optional paragraph 1:** Briefly explain why the situation occurred. Include names, dates, and reasons as appropriate.)*

*(**Optional paragraph 2:** Explain restitution proceedings and disciplinary actions planned, as appropriate.)*

Once again, please accept our sincere apology for *(brief definition of problem)*. If such things occur again or if you experience any other inconveniences involving this company, please call me personally at *(direct or personal telephone line number)*. We will correct the situation immediately.

Very sincerely yours,

Signature

Name
Title

7b. APOLOGIES—ADMITTING ERROR

Date

Name/Title
Business/Organization Name
Address
City, State ZIP

Dear (*name*):

People do not like to admit they are wrong, but apparently you caught us with egg on our face. We are ashamed to admit it, but you are absolutely right. Those are powdered eggs in our Denver omelets. The waitress who told you otherwise was either misinformed or incorrect.

I spoke to the chef, who admits that in blind taste tests held at a recent food trade show, he was unable to detect any difference between the powdered eggs and the real thing. Further, he said, there are distinct dietary advantages to the powdered variety in terms of reduced fats and cholesterol. All in all, he felt the powdered eggs were a better choice. Apparently, however, you did not.

Taste is a personal issue, but the menu did present the omelets as if we used real eggs. We are sorry for the miscommunication. The error in advertising, if not in culinary judgment, was ours. We would like to make it up to you. Enclosed you will find a coupon for a complimentary meal for two, good on any selection any time of the day.

And this time, we will make the chef use real eggs. I guarantee it personally. Thank you for helping us do a better job serving our customers.

Best regards,

Signature

Name
Title

7C. APOLOGIES—REDIRECTING BLAME

Date

Name/Title
Business/Organization Name
Address
City, State ZIP

Dear (*name*):

Sales manager Claude Lenz brought to our attention the problem you are having with the tractor drive on the two Quantum Leap computer printers in your Eastdale office. I am the technician who analyzed the printers the last time you had trouble and prescribed what I thought would be the appropriate solution.

Quantum Leap makes a full line of fine products, but we have noted in the past year that the tractor drives on several models of their XJ1 printers have been malfunctioning. In some cases, the pins that grip the paper snap off; in others, the roller becomes too loose in its carriage to effectively advance the paper. We have serviced many recently, but we stopped using these parts as of last November, when Quantum ordered a recall of the product.

In checking with Quantum, it appears that the Korean supplier responsible for that particular mechanism has been experiencing severe quality control problems. Quantum has stopped dealing with that supplier and assures us that future tractor feeds on all its printers will work properly.

Given the situation and our warning at the time of repair, we feel we are not obligated to repair the printer a second time at no charge. This is clearly a problem in manufacturing, and will not be rectified by anything we do. Our Quantum Leap representative, Cynthia Chow, has asked that all inquiries be directed to her. Her telephone number is (800) 555-1234.

If there is anything else we can do, please let us know.

Best wishes,

Signature

Name
Title

8a. APPOINTMENTS—REQUESTING

Date

Name/Title
Business/Organization Name
Address
City, State ZIP

Dear (*name*):

If you have a free hour, I can show you a way to reduce the sorting and route management costs of your delivery business by up to 65 percent. Interested?

Those of us in the delivery business know that a fast sort of parcels and correspondence can make or break delivery time promises. Yet our greatest challenge is finding a sorting method that is fast, error-free, and relatively inexpensive. TimeSplits is offering a new technology that can help you solve your sorting problems without an expensive reengineering of your operation.

TimeSplits' new ZIP Sort adapts to existing routing systems while making use of basic personal computer technology to log, track, and route packages, parcels, and letters to both hub and isolated destinations. What's more, it reduces rather than increases dependence on staff to hand-sort misfiled items.

If you can spare an hour during the week of August 16, I can show you a way to improve service while reducing costs. I guarantee it will be one of the best hours you will spend all year.

I will call next week to set up an appointment where we can discuss your needs in more detail. The future of mail and package sorting has arrived, and I would like you to be among the first to take advantage of this new technology.

Sincerely,

Signature

Name
Title

8b. Appointments—Requesting (Personal)

MEMORANDUM

TO: Vice President/Personnel
FROM: Vice President/Operations
DATE:
SUBJECT: The Task You Hate Most

I am going to need a moment of your time next week, Ed. Make that 30 minutes. After much coaching, encouragement, and support, I believe I am going to have to pull the plug on John Lipscomb. Even after an extensive probation period, John still lacks the ability, the will, or some combination of the two to perform satisfactory work. My department no longer can support him.

I know this is the task you hate most, Ed. It is not easy for me, either, but it's best for the company. He is not holding to his part of the bargain, and we are not doing him any favors by keeping him on when there is no future for him here.

I'll be in Atlanta through Wednesday of next week. Can we get together Thursday morning at 9:30 to review the personnel files and talk about the best way to handle John? The sooner we take care of this, the better for all concerned.

Thanks for your help on this one, Ed.

8c. Appointments—Acknowledging

Date

Name/Title
Business/Organization Name
Address
City, State ZIP

Dear (*name*):

Your staff has acknowledged receipt of our request to audit your books for the second quarter of this year. Their suggested appointment dates of March 14–16 at your corporate headquarters on Delancy Street are agreeable.

While we will not require constant staff access to anyone other than your chief financial officer, we do request a preliminary meeting with your executive management staff prior to starting the audit. A time of 8 a.m. to 9:30 a.m. on March 14 is preferable for us. If this is inconvenient for some reason, contact David Sullivan immediately to reschedule the appointment.

We assume all books and records will be in order. You may have legal counsel present at the preliminary meeting if you so desire. Any questions should be directed to Mr. Sullivan.

Sincerely,
Signature
Name
Title

8d. Appointments—Acknowledging (Personal)

Date

Name/Title
Business/Organization Name
Address
City, State ZIP

Dear (*name*):

Your message came through loud and clear. I will be happy to discuss your future plans, goals, and needs with you on June 6. Your office is fine, as is the time of 7:30 p.m.

Despite our long-standing friendship, I think this meeting is one for which we both need to prepare. I have got some ideas about directions you might take, but I want to hear what you think. I suggest you look inside—as deeply as possible—and ask yourself what it is you really want for yourself as a member of our firm. Think about what you like doing and what you are really good at. That will form a good basis for our talk.

I look forward to meeting with you.

Sincerely,
Signature
Name
Title

8e. Appointments—Declining

Date

Name/Title
Business/Organization Name
Address
City, State ZIP

Dear (*name*):

On May 31, we received your letter requesting an appointment with our client, Pennsylvania Matchlocks Inc. After conferring with principals of the firm, we regret to inform you that we must respectfully decline your request.

Mr. Taylor Prince, president of Pennsylvania Matchlocks Inc., has informed us that his firm is no longer interested in doing business with Hookline & Sinker Inc. What's more, Mr. Prince has retained our office to consider legal proceedings against your firm. To date, no action has been taken, but we are reviewing options.

We will be in touch in the near future concerning the matter of the missing shipment. Until then, we will decline all future requests for an appointment.

Sincerely,
Signature
Name
Title

8f. APPOINTMENTS—POSTPONING

Date

Name/Title
Business/Organization Name
Address
City, State ZIP

Dear (*name*):

Mr. Thrush regrets that he was called home to New York to attend to pressing personal business and will not be available for your noon luncheon appointment this coming Friday. He has asked me to reschedule the meeting.

Your secretary, Robin, has informed me that you have an opening two weeks from Wednesday at 3:00 p.m. She has already rescheduled the appointment for Mr. Thrush at that time. If this is inconvenient, please contact either me or Mr. Starling immediately.

We regret any inconvenience this may have caused. Mr. Thrush appreciates your patience and flexibility.

Kindest regards,

Signature

Name
Title

8g. APPOINTMENTS—POSTPONING (PERSONAL)

Date

Name/Title
Business/Organization Name
Address
City, State ZIP

Dear (*name*):

Welcome back to the USA! No doubt your overseas negotiations were exhausting, and I am sure you are glad to be back on familiar soil. You deserve a rest, and I plan to help you.

Actually, that is just a clever way to say I am going to have to postpone our February 14 appointment for at least two weeks. After my Valentine's Day obligations, I am off to Seattle to conduct a week-long workshop, followed by some business appointments in Portland and Boise. I know I will be worn out after that, so I am taking four days of R&R in Aspen.

I would like to reschedule the appointment for February 28, if that's OK with you. Same time, same place. If that won't work, have Shelly call Monica to set up a time when we're both available.

See you soon,

Signature

Name

8h. Appointments—Regrets for a Missed Appointment (Business)

Date
Name/Title
Business/Organization Name
Address
City, State ZIP

Dear (*name*):

Please accept our apologies for not appearing at the meeting of your executive board last week to formally present our bid as a supplier on your new project. Mr. Hruby called from the accident site on his cellular telephone before he was taken to the hospital, and we attempted to contact you. Unfortunately, you and your board already had begun the meeting, and the secretary was unable or unwilling to interrupt. By the time Ms. Seekins arrived to fill in for Mr. Hruby, the meeting already had disbanded, and the principals had left.

Despite the unavoidable nature of the situation, we feel there is no excuse for having inconvenienced your executives, and we respectfully withdraw our bid for the project. If you wish to reopen negotiations, we will be glad to do so. But we will understand completely if you decide to go with another supplier.

Again, please accept the heartfelt regrets of Mr. Hruby, Ms. Seekins, and the principals of our firm.

Sincerely,

Signature

Name
Title

9a. APPRECIATION—TO ACCOMPANY AWARDS, HONORS, AND RECOGNITION

Date

Name/Title
Business/Organization Name
Address
City, State ZIP

Dear (*name*):

In too many situations, it is only the squeaky wheels that get the grease. But I am pleased to see that recognition also comes to the well-oiled, most smoothly operating machines.

Congratulations on your recent Directors Award! The news about your honor was barely out before people began commenting that it was about time your high performance was noticed. We couldn't be more happy for you.

The honor speaks well of your commitment to our industry. In addition to echoing the accolade, we would like to tender our thanks for the personal contributions you have made, as well as those for which you are being publicly recognized. Automotive parts and service is a competitive game. Your contributions have made everyone's job easier.

Sincerely,

Signature

Name
Title

9b. APPRECIATION—FOR PROMOTION

MEMORANDUM

TO: District Sales Manager
FROM: Vice President/Sales
DATE:
SUBJECT: Congratulations!

Now that the champagne glasses are empty and the shouting has died down, let me congratulate you on your recent promotion to District Sales Manager. When Gordy left us so suddenly, we hoped one of you would stand out as the likely successor. We're glad and not surprised to see that it was you, (*name*).

Your contributions over the years to (*company name*) have helped us rise in the ranks of the small arms industry. Your task now is to take us over the top. This won't be easy, but we are confident we have the right person to do the job.

We have appreciated your efforts, (*name*), and hope this promotion provides the incentive you need to hit all the targets at which you're aiming. Good luck and, again, congratulations!

9c. APPRECIATION—FOR ADDED EFFORT, ASSISTANCE

MEMORANDUM

TO: Vice President/Personnel
FROM: Manager/Parts Department
DATE:
SUBJECT: Thanks for the Assist!

Job cutbacks are never an easy thing to deal with, (*name*). The most recent round, while financially necessary, was particularly devastating to staff morale. From what I heard, most employees spent the last ninety days wondering if they would be the next ones to get a pink slip.

Despite that, the people in your department pitched in like they never had before. If anything, the stress and strain of the past few months seem to have brought your staff closer together, and your contributions to the new streamlined company format have been magnificent. (*Name*), delivery systems manager, told me she was particularly appreciative of your flexibility and the informal staff "lend/lease" program you developed to help her out.

Those kinds of contributions are what makes (*name of company*) an industry leader. I just wanted to echo the feelings of President (*name*) that I, too, greatly appreciate the contributions of your team.

9d. Appreciation—For Supporting an Idea (Personal)

Date:

(Name of employee):

Just a short note to thank you for your support on the *(identifying name)* proposal. That was a tough room to play, with no one giving any quarter on anything. Even rational arguments and solid facts were not enough to help *(name)* get his idea across. I was having the same struggle until you, *(name 1)*, and *(name 2)* all voiced your support. I think that made the difference in getting the proposal approved.

The *(client company)* people are very happy, and so am I. Thanks again for the vital support. I hope I can return the favor.

9e. Appreciation—For an Interview

Date

Name/Title
Business/Organization Name
Address
City, State ZIP

Dear *(name)*:

Time to a busy executive is a valuable commodity. Thank you for sharing so much of yours last Tuesday, helping me examine how I might best serve in achieving the mission of *(name of company)*.

Few job interviews have been as informative as the hour I spent with you, and few opportunities have left me feeling as exhilarated. My background in drainage systems and storm water runoff management provides me with skills I believe mesh well with your company's purpose and tasks. I am eager to put them to work serving your clients.

Thanks again for the time. I have got my sleeves rolled up and am ready to start whenever you are.

Sincerely,
Signature
Name

9f. APPRECIATION—PERSONAL

(Name of employee):

This has been a tough week. Frankly, I never thought I would survive, but then I didn't know what a strong shoulder to cry on you have. Thank you for being there and for never asking any questions, never making any judgments, and never running out of tissues.

(Name), a former coworker of mine, says there are no true Good Samaritans left. Some day I will have to introduce the two of you to show her how wrong she is.

9g. APPRECIATION—GENERIC

Date

Name/Title
Business/Organization Name
Address
City, State ZIP

Dear *(name)*:

Too often, good efforts go unrecognized. I want to personally thank you for *(identify issue and support provided)*.

*(**Optional Paragraph 1:** Offer details or background of the issue and explain how the recipient's support helped address challenges.)*

*(**Optional Paragraph 2:** Extrapolate from the present to how the support provided will affect future activities or scenarios.)*

In today's world, support freely given is a rare commodity. I'm glad I was able to find a little light in the growing social darkness. Thanks again for your help.

Sincerely,
Signature
Name
Title

10a. Bids—Soliciting

Date

Name/Title
Business/Organization Name
Address
City, State ZIP

Dear (*name*):

The Office of Thrift Supervision (OTS) invites bids on several former savings and loan associations of which it has seized the assets and assumed ownership. The association have an aggregate $14 billion in assets and are located in affluent suburbs of Los Angeles, CA; Phoenix, AZ; and Dallas, TX.

We will accept confidential bids in writing through August 31. Each association will be considered an independent unit for sale, but bidders may include bids on all five properties in one sealed envelope. We will award properties to the highest bidder, pending proven ability to gain financing.

A complete prospectus for each savings and loan association is available by writing the Dallas office of OTS, which is responsible for liquidation. We will notify winning bidders within one week of the close of bidding. Nonwinners will be notified within two weeks.

Sincerely,

Signature

Name
Title

10b. BIDS—ACCEPTING

Date
Name/Title
Business/Organization Name
Address
City, State ZIP

Dear (*name*):

The officers of Bonebreak Clinic are pleased to accept your bid for providing regular diagnostic services and cancer screening through your comprehensive facility at Meredith Hospital.

Many excellent providers approached clinic physician and administrative staff, but none showed the sensitivity to our purpose that you have. Your rates, while not the lowest, certainly are competitive. But our main concern is the welfare of our patients. We feel you have demonstrated competence and compassion in the services you offer. We are pleased to welcome you to our medical family.

(Name) will be in touch shortly concerning financial and operational arrangements. Your contracts will be turned over to clinic manager *(name)*, who will handle all further business arrangements.

We look forward to our growing relationship in better serving the patients of *(names)* counties.

Sincerely,

Signature

Name
Title

10c. BIDS—REJECTING

Date
Name/Title
Business/Organization Name
Address
City, State ZIP

Dear *(name)*:

We regret to inform you that your bid to provide chlorination and chemical services for pools and fountains of *(city name)* has not met our expectations based on previous informal discussions we have had. Thus, we must reject your bid until it approaches a price more within our budget.

(Name) had initial discussions with your staff the week of *(date)* and again two weeks later. At the time, *(name)*, your representative, indicated that annual chlorination and chemical service for *(city)*'s three swimming pools and sixteen civic fountains would be "in the neighborhood of $60,000." Your written bid of $342,000 far exceeds those preliminary expectations.

We suggest you talk to *(name)*, as well as rethink your proposition. Public water season starts in less than sixty days. If we have not arrived at an agreement by April 10, we will have to seek those services elsewhere.

Your immediate attention to this matter is vital.

Sincerely,

Signature

Name
Title

11a. Billing Errors—Alerting Customer to the Error

Date

Name/Title
Business/Organization Name
Address
City, State ZIP

Dear (*name*):

Our accounting department has noted a serious error in the billing of your recent order for carpeting. In computing the total amount, sales representative *(name)* failed to include the estimates given you for two of the bedrooms. Our bid of $1,800 was seriously in error. The true cost of the carpeting is $2,600. A new invoice is attached.

We sincerely regret any inconvenience *(name)*'s error has caused you. We pride ourselves on being the area's low-price carpet leader, but I'm afraid *(name)* overstepped the bounds a little bit.

We appreciate your down payment of $1,000 and request that the new balance due of $1,600 be paid within thirty days. Again, we apologize for the confusion and appreciate your business.

Sincerely,

Signature

Name
Title

11b. BILLING ERRORS—ALERTING BUSINESS TO THE ERROR

Date

Name/Title
Business/Organization Name
Address
City, State ZIP

Dear (*name*):

Your recent bill of $142.32 mystifies us. Surely past telephone bills indicate that we make frequent calls to Maine, Florida, and Oklahoma. But we are at a loss to explain three successive calls to Taipei, Taiwan and four calls to Sydney, Australia on May 6 and 8, respectively.

Rest assured no one in this house made them. We can only consider them another instance of computer error or, perhaps, fraud. Whatever the reason, we would like them removed from our bill. Our enclosed check does not include payment for these charges.

Thanks for your attention to this matter.

Best regards,

Signature

Name

11c. BILLING ERRORS—CORRECTING BUYER'S ERROR

Date

Name/Title
Business/Organization Name
Address
City, State ZIP

Dear (*name*):

Nobody's perfect. We here at Discount Motors know that as well as the next person, and we are sure your error in the order and prepayment for the Baby Moon hubcaps for your vintage '57 Chevrolet Bel Air was unintentional.

We realized only after the fact that the catalogue and price that you showed to (*name*) in the parts department, was actually that of a competitor, Hi-Power Auto Sales. When we checked the order, we found that the price in our most recent catalogue was actually 15 percent higher than the price you prepaid (*name*) before ordering.

We're sorry for the mixup, but we're happy to tell you that your Baby Moons have arrived. If you will pay (*name*) the difference between the actual price and what you paid, he will be happy to install them personally.

Yours in motoring,

Signature

Name
Title

11d. Billing Errors—Correcting Seller's Error

Date

Name/Title
Business/Organization Name
Address
City, State ZIP

Dear (*name*):

The chair we purchased recently arrived balance due. When we again checked the newspaper ad and the price you advertised, we realize there must be some mix-up.

According to the ad, the original price of the chair was $299, marked down to $199 for your annual "going out of business" sale. When your delivery man wheeled in the chair, he presented a C.O.D. bill for $100, plus sales tax and a $25 delivery charge. When we bought the chair, you told us that the $199 price included delivery.

When we refused to pay, the delivery man left with the chair. Needless to say, we are disappointed and want either our chair or our payment returned immediately. Please call and let us know what you are going to do.

Sincerely,

Signature

Name

11e. Billing Errors—Restitution

Date

Name/Title
Business/Organization Name
Address
City, State ZIP

Dear (*name*):

Please accept our apology in the mix-up over your recent chair purchase. You were right and our billing department was wrong. They lost the sales file on this purchase and reverted to basic procedure for the item. The delivery man was only doing what he was instructed to do in such situations.

By now your chair should have been returned to you and the account settled. If that hasn't happened, please call me immediately and I will see to the delivery personally. There is no excuse for any further mix-up.

By way of restitution, please accept this coupon for 15% off your next furniture purchase. This coupon will be honored for all full- and sale-priced items except spas and hot tubs, which we subcontract from another distributor. We also have added you to our Customer Gold list, which will enable you to preview all items prior to their going on advertised sale.

Again, please accept our apology for this mix-up. We thank you for your continued business.

Warm regards,

Signature

Name
Title

12a. CLAIMS—INSURANCE (GENERIC)

Date
Name/Title
Business/Organization Name
Address
City, State ZIP

Dear (*name*):

On (*date*), our company suffered a (*name or nature of mishap*) that damaged or destroyed (*approximate extent of damage, either in scope or financial approximation*). This damage and loss is covered by your comprehensive business policy no. (*number of policy*).

(*Optional paragraph #1: Detail the nature of the loss, including valuables and irreplaceables that may have been covered by the policy.*)

(*Optional paragraph #2: Detail the business need for promptness, e.g., deadlines or payrolls to meet.*)

We need your immediate attention to this matter. A quick settlement will allow us to start the necessary restoration and once again begin serving our customers.

Thank you for your assistance.

Sincerely,

Signature

Name
Title

12b. CLAIMS—ERROR IN CLAIM

Date
Name/Title
Business/Organization Name
Address
City, State ZIP

Dear (*name*):

Your insurance adjuster, *(name)*, recently submitted the assessment and the check for the wind damage to our roof. There are specific errors within the claim that you need to address.

The damage was to the dormer on the north side of the house. High winds from last month's storms had lifted many of the tiles from the roof and caused a leak. This caused water damage to the internal ceiling of an upstairs bedroom. When *(name)* examined the dormer, he looked only at the roofing on the dormer's south side, where damage was minimal. The true damage was on the north side. *(Name)* awarded damages based on what he saw, and it seems that he did not look very closely at the extent of the damage.

A specialist from Caesar Roofing estimates repairs to both the roof and the water-damaged ceiling at $968. Your check for $232 arrived today. I am holding the check until I receive your response to this letter. Please contact me as soon as possible about this matter.

Sincerely,

Signature

Name

12c. Claims—Response to Challenge [Positive]

Date

Name/Title
Address
City, State ZIP

Dear (*name*):

We have reviewed your recent letter and challenge to *(name)*'s assessment of your claim. We agree that he made a mistake.

We apologize for any inconvenience this may have caused you. We will be sending a new adjuster to review the damage to your roof and ceiling. Since your letter clearly outlines the nature of the damage, we will send it along with the adjuster. We would appreciate it if you could show him where the damage occurred.

I am confident we can rectify the situation in a way satisfactory to both of us. We appreciate your patience in this matter. Rest assured that our adjuster will call within forty-eight hours to schedule an appointment convenient for you.

Sincerely,

Signature

Name
Title

12d. CLAIMS—RESPONSE TO CHALLENGE (NEGATIVE)

Date
Name/Title
Business/Organization Name
Address
City, State ZIP

Dear (*name*):

Thank you for your recent correspondence regarding (*name*)'s assessment and
evaluation of the wind damage to your roof. We also have reviewed (*name*)'s notes
and Polaroid snapshots and are satisfied that the adjustment he made is in keeping
with both the damage done and the policy requirements.

Different repair firms estimate the cost of repairs by different standards. We use a
national firm based in Atlanta to evaluate the nature and replacement costs for such
damage. Their assessments, adjusted geographically, reflect what we feel are
average and reasonable costs. Those costs have been applied to your specific case.

We're sorry you do not feel adequately compensated, but a review of your policy
shows a $250 deductible. When this is added to the amount our firm sent you, the
total represents the average cost for roof repair for homes in your area.

If you have any further questions, please contact me personally.

Sincerely,

Signature

Name
Title

12e. CLAIMS—REQUEST FOR RESTITUTION

Date
Name/Title
Business/Organization Name
Address
City, State ZIP

Dear (*name*):

Not all things turn out as well as they look. Such was the case with the temporary employee you sent our accounting department last Wednesday to Friday, July 6-8. Charming as *(name)* was, she had little background in office practice, much less accounting, and proved to make more work for our accounting manager, not less. That is the reverse of what we usually expect.

Given our long relationship, we thought perhaps we had been mistaken, but in the cold light of the following day, it is clear that the problem lay with someone else. We would hate to think it was your firm, but we cannot believe you would have been taken in by *(name)*. In any case, we were less than satisfied with the experience.

We find your bill of $188 for *(name)*'s service unacceptable, given her performance, and we expect to pay nothing for the three days of confusion she caused in our offices. Your agreement will enable us to continue our historically good working relationship.

Sincerely,

Signature

Name
Title

12f. CLAIMS—RESPONSE TO RESTITUTION CLAIM

Date

Name/Title
Business/Organization Name
Address
City, State ZIP

Dear (*name*):

Capable. Competent. Knowledgeable. Eager. We would be delighted to have her back.

Those are comments from the last four appraisals of *(name)*. None of our past clients who worked with this particular associate seem to have had any trouble with her. As a matter of fact, *(name)* recently left our employment to take a position with a firm with which she worked as a temporary. For the record, it was one of the larger accounting firms in Harvest Town.

That is not to say that your perceptions were not accurate. We all have bad days, and perhaps *(name)* had several when working for your firm. In the interest of a continued good working relationship, we agree to cancel our invoice for her services.

We apologize for the problem and look forward to serving your temporary employee needs in the future.

Very truly yours,

Signature

Name
Title

13a. COMMENDATIONS—TO PRESIDING CHAIRMAN OR OFFICIAL

Date

Name/Title
Business/Organization Name
Address
City, State ZIP

Dear (*name*):

The annual meeting at Desert Wells came off without a hitch, *(first name)*, and that is a tribute to the staff and officials who worked so hard to put it together. It is also due to your leadership, moderating influence, and hosting abilities demonstrated during the three-day event. I don't think I have ever been kept so closely to a clock and schedule. Thanks for your "timely" influence.

As you know, I have worked for numerous chairmen supervising a multitude of directors. Some were better than others, but few measured up to you in ability and influence. I have appreciated your hard work and mentoring over the past two years, *(first name)*, and will be truly sorry when your term comes to an end. The organization has grown and prospered significantly under your influence, and so have I.

Kindest regards,

Signature

Name
Title

13b. COMMENDATIONS—FOR ASSISTANCE

Date

Name/Title
Business/Organization Name
Address
City, State ZIP

Dear (*name*):

Many thanks for the loan of (*name*) during our recent staff shortage. It is easy to see why you consider her your right-hand person, and we are surprised you were able to function without her for the past three weeks.

If ever anyone had an intuitive sense for spotting office problems before they occur, it must be (*name*). She headed off several potential crises, both major and minor, and finally helped us fix the photocopier that had been giving us so many problems. Even (*name*), our copier repairman, was pleasantly surprised.

We appreciate your generosity and return (*name*) to you with our most sincere appreciation, and the utmost regret that you are a good enough friend to lend her to us in the first place. If you were not, we would steal her in a heartbeat.

Thanks again, (*name*). You are a lifesaver.

Warm regards,

Signature

Name
Title

13c. COMMENDATIONS—FOR INTERNAL ASSISTANCE

MEMORANDUM

TO: Marketing
FROM: President
DATE:
SUBJECT: Your Recent Assistance

As you know, *(first name)*, I am most impressed by staff people who not only can get things done, but also are not afraid to pitch in for others when the need arises. That is all part of National Demographics' teamwork approach, and I was pleased to see that you were not afraid to do your part.

No, strike that. Clearly, you and *(name)* did much more than your parts, particularly when *(name)* was taken ill. I am used to being one of the last ones out the door at night, and it was a pleasant surprise to see the marketing team hard at work, tackling tasks that were not officially even theirs to do.

I plan to report the results of this past quarter at Friday's staff meeting, but I wanted you and *(name)* to know first that we not only did not lose any ground while *(name)* was out, but actually picked up sixteen new accounts. That is due entirely to the hard work of the two of you.

Good show! My hat's off to you.

13d. COMMENDATIONS—GENERIC

Date

Name/Title
Business/Organization Name
Address
City, State ZIP

Dear (*name*):

Today's market places high demands on people to perform to ever higher standards. I am pleased to say that, thanks to your recent effort on (*name, description of project, effort*), you have exceeded our standards and expectations.

(***Optional paragraph #1:*** *Outline superior performance in light of job or task requirements.*)

(***Optional paragraph #2:*** *Outline the favorable impact the effort has had on company goals or initiatives.*)

(*Name of supervisor*) said we could count on your hard work and superior results, but even (*he/she*) would be surprised by the effect your assistance has had. Thank you for your effort. You have shown us that the work ethic is not only alive, but healthier than ever.

With warm regards,

Signature

Name
Title

14a. COMPLAINTS—TO SUBORDINATES

MEMORANDUM

TO:
FROM:
DATE:

(Name):

Correct me if I'm wrong, but isn't it your department's policy to complete all tasks before ending your work day? Several customer inquiries came in yesterday after the last of your crew had left, and those remaining from other departments could not answer them. That made us appear incompetent in the eyes of some of our most important customers.

I know it is difficult to plan for these last-minute calls, but it should be standard operating procedure to have at least one member of your staff on hand during business hours. There has been a complete absence of staff over several lunch periods as well, and I think we are setting a bad precedent here.

Please make sure your department is adequately staffed during all business hours. We are a service organization, and we can't provide that service if we're not here to deliver it, can we?

14b. COMPLAINTS—TO PEERS

MEMORANDUM

TO:
FROM:
DATE:

(Name):

In spite of recent administrative mandates, I have noticed an almost complete lack of cooperation and assistance between your staff and mine.

In the past, we have lived with this. But now that we have a staff hiring freeze and everyone's workload has increased by 30 percent, better cooperation is not only preferable but vital. We cannot get along without each other, no matter how much we might try.

(Name) and I would like to meet with you and *(name)* to discuss what we can do to improve relations. How about 12:30 at Dominick's? Lunch will be on us.

14c. Complaints—To Superiors

M E M O R A N D U M

TO:
FROM:
DATE:

(*Name*):

To develop a better working relationship with our printers and typesetters in Cincinnati during our annual convention, we will need to provide half the estimated printing costs up front in the form of a certified check. This has nothing to do with our credit record. It is simply a matter of their policy in dealing with out-of-town groups.

Unfortunately, (*name*) refuses to produce the necessary check because she says it is against company policy. Under most circumstances, I would agree, but she fails to recognize the special needs of this situation. Her delay is costing us precious time in completing the printing we will need for the convention.

Will you please talk to (*name*) and assure her that it is okay to honor our request? Without it, you can kiss the convention program books goodbye. And I am sure that is not something either you or I care to tell our president.

14d. COMPLAINTS—TO COMPETITORS

Date

Name/Title
Business/Organization Name
Address
City, State ZIP

Dear (*name*):

It looks to us like you may have really put your foot in it this time, and we are not above asking for legal assistance in getting a cease-and-desist order. But let's try it the friendly way first.

Your recent shopper ad offers direct comparisons to our firm, claiming rates we do not offer, service problems not characteristic of us, and customer complaints we were not privy to. In the spoken word, that type of false and damaging information is called slander. When it appears in print, it is libel. And we want it stopped.

If the ad in question ever appears anywhere again, our attorney is prepared to file a libel suit immediately. If it does not reappear, we are willing to drop the whole thing. But we also would advise you not to make this a habit. Some competitors are even more vehement about such things than we are and may not give you fair warning.

Regards,

Signature

Name
Title

14e. COMPLAINTS—TO OPPONENTS

Date

Name/Title
Business/Organization Name
Address
City, State ZIP

Dear (*name*):

My campaign manager and I saw your comments about the upcoming election in the leading industry trade journal and wonder what "dirt" you think you might have that you think would cause me to pull out of this election in the 11th hour?

Preliminary polls already are in, and it looks like you are favored to win. But my constituency has yet to be counted, and I would appreciate it if you would keep your fabricated stories about moral turpitude to yourself. You have no proof, and even if you manufacture someone who claims to have been my paramour, my background will do as much to refute that as anything else.

It appears that some politicians do not mind being cast in that light, but, frankly, I do not like it. So please stop it, unless you are ready to prove your contention in a court of law.

Sincere regards,

Signature

Name
Title

14f. COMPLAINTS—FOR POOR PRODUCT/SERVICE

Date

Name/Title
Business/Organization Name
Address
City, State ZIP

Dear (*name*):

On December 17, we requested that your electronics firm provide our company with cable and modem access for the purpose of communications with our branch offices. The cabling came, along with your rather hefty bill, but the communications did not. After six weeks and twice as many telephone calls to your firm, we still do not have an active network. And we are tired of waiting.

We know that on-line communication will help us operate more efficiently. Each day we are without it costs us money. Thus, we demand that you send in capable service technicians immediately to rectify the situation.

We are also holding your bill and will not make payment until the system works. The sooner you rectify the situation, the sooner we will pay. It's that simple.

Regards,

Signature

Name
Title

15a. CONDOLENCES—DEATH (BUSINESS EPITAPH)

Some entrepreneurs are known for their successes, others for their heart. But few are known for the ability to accomplish great feats and their willingness to go out of their way on behalf of other people. *(Name)* was just such a man, and he will be sorely missed by the community he served.

(First name) was never too big to talk to the kids on the street, the ones just getting by who need more than a helping hand. He was never too proud to pull off his sport coat and help push a problem out of the way, no matter how big it was. And he was never too small not to be able to see the other guy's point of view, no matter how different it may have been from his.

(First name) was truly a special person. The loss of his helping hand and big smile is a tragedy for those of us whose lives he touched, and who were lucky enough to count him among our friends.

15b. CONDOLENCES—DEATH (BUSINESS)

Date

Name/Title
Business/Organization name
Address
City, State, ZIP

Dear *(name)*:

On behalf of the staff at *(name of company)*, please accept our sincere condolences over the loss of *(name of person)*. She was an able leader and a wonderful woman. Her presence and influence will be sorely missed.

Sincerely,

Signature

Name
Title

15c. CONDOLENCES—DEATH [PERSONAL]

Date

(Name):

I guess some of us knew it was coming, but even the best planning never prepares you for the loss of a loved one. Please accept our deepest sympathies over the passing of *(first name of deceased)*. We loved him dearly, and will miss him greatly.

(First name of deceased) meant a lot to us, both because of his warm, giving nature and because of his ability to step forward in almost any crisis. *(Name)* will never forget the help and strength *(first name of deceased)* gave him when his business was in trouble. I was *(name)*'s heart during that time, but *(first name of deceased)* was his fortitude. Without *(first name of deceased)*'s support, I do not think *(name)* would have come back as well as he did. What *(name)* is today he owes as much to *(first name of deceased)* as to anyone else.

During times like these, we have to work through our pain. But if there is anything either *(name)* or I can do to help ease yours, please call us. Day or night, we are here for you.

Love,
Signature

15d. CONDOLENCES—SYMPATHY

Date

Name/Title
Business/Organization Name
Address
City, State ZIP

Dear *(name):*

(Name)'s accident did not exactly make the headlines, but those of us at The Paint Store who knew him by the little hop he did when he entered the shop will miss him as he recuperates from that fall he took from the second story of the Gregg Building.

To a man like *(name)*, a little pain won't slow him down. But we are sure that three weeks of inactivity and another two weeks of therapy and limited movement will be like going to prison. If there is anything we can do during his convalescence, we hope you will call.

Best regards,

Signature

Name
Title

16a. CONFIRMATION—OF APPOINTMENT

Date

Name/Title
Business/Organization Name
Address
City, State ZIP

Dear *(name)*:

This note confirms the appointment you made with Mr. *(name)* for Tuesday, January 12, at 1:30 p.m. The meeting will take place in the executive dining room at Blackstar's, and also will involve Ms. *(name)* and Mr. *(name)*.

Mr. *(name)* requests that you bring the full scope of your proposal to the table at this meeting, including architectural renderings of the new structures. The more detail you have to answer questions, the more likely it is that you will interest him in the project.

Please understand that this is not a formal request for proposal. Mr. *(Name)* has heard a great deal about your work and is intrigued by many of the ideas your architecture represents. If the meeting goes well, Mr. *(name)* may invite you to make a more formal presentation to the partners at Century Enterprises.

Sincerely,

Signature

Name
Title

16b. Confirmation—Of an Appointment to a New Job

Date

Name/Title
Business/Organization Name
Address
City, State ZIP

Dear *(name)*:

No doubt you are still basking in the glory, *(name)*, but let me put it in writing for the permanent record. This note confirms your appointment as team leader for Octagon Inc.'s new quality management effort. Congratulations!

The board of directors would not have selected you had it not been impressed by the scope and nature of your work. Tapping you for the position was one big shot in the arm for both *(name)* and Octagon. I know we will all prosper by working together.

Your first task will be to appoint a team of advisers to head the various facets of our new quality initiatives, one for each of the six categories. Then, under your direction, those six will begin building their quality teams and setting goals. That is step number two.

As for step number three . . . well, that is what you have been appointed to develop. Good luck, and please call if I can be of any assistance.

Best regards,

Signature

Name
Title

16c. CONFIRMATION—OF ATTENDANCE

Date

Name/Title
Business/Organization Name
Address
City, State ZIP

Dear *(name):*

This letter confirms your attendance at the Management Workshop scheduled for September 9–13 at the Sheraton Royale in downtown Toronto, Ontario. The sessions run from 8:30 a.m. to 4:30 p.m. each of the five days. There will be a cocktail reception Monday evening from 6:00 p.m. to 7:30 p.m.

Please be sure to review the enclosed course material prior to Monday's opening session. Familiarity with the case study will increase your learning experience and enhance class participation. That gives us all a head start toward a more productive session.

You must make hotel arrangements on your own using the attached forms. Be sure to mention that you will be attending the Management Workshop to receive the most favorable rate. If you have any questions or require any further assistance, please don't hesitate to call. Otherwise, we'll see you in Toronto.

Kindest regards,

Signature

Name
Title

16d. CONFIRMATION—OF AN HONOR

Date

Name/Title
Business/Organization name
Address
City, State ZIP

Dear *(name)*:

Many are called but few are chosen, as the saying goes. We are happy to inform you that you were one of those chosen by our judging panel, and that your annual report has been selected to receive a first place Gold Award in our marketing competition. Congratulations!

All first-place winners will be publicly announced at the upcoming Leadership Symposium scheduled for April 12-15 at Kiawah Island Resort. We are keeping it a secret until then. But we hope you will be able to attend the symposium and enjoy the recognition and honor you deserve for your outstanding work.

We have attached registration materials, and planned a special luncheon to announce all winning attendees. We look forward to seeing you there.

Again, congratulations on your Gold Award! It is an achievement of which you and your staff can be very proud.

Best regards,

Signature

Name
Title

17a. Congratulations—Generic

Date

Name/Title
Business/Organization Name
Address
City, State ZIP

Dear *(name):*

Good news doesn't stay a secret long. We would like to extend our heartiest congratulations for *(name of honor or event).* It is reassuring to know that those who
work so hard achieve the recognition they deserve. We are very pleased for you.

*(**Optional paragraph:** Detail the conditions surrounding the award, or special reasons why the recipient is particularly deserving.)*

Congratulations again on your *(brief identification of honor).* We cannot think of a
more deserving person.

Sincerely,

Signature

Name

17b. CONGRATULATIONS—PROMOTION

Date

Name/Title
Business/Organization Name
Address
City, State ZIP

Dear *(name):*

Our business relationship with Confab Industries over the past five years has been both profitable and pleasurable, and no one has contributed more to that than you. Thus, we are delighted to send our congratulations on your promotion to vice president.

Before the new administration took over, Confab was floundering with little market presence. You helped turn it around and make it one of the real powerhouses of the plastic injection molding business. We are pleased to see that those in charge also were aware of your contributions.

We hope you will accept and enjoy the enclosed bottle of champagne with our compliments. Although we cannot be with you in person, we wanted to be among the first to toast your continued success.

Kindest regards,

Signature

Name
Title

17c. Congratulations—Awards/Honors

Date

Name/Title
Business/Organization Name
Address
City, State ZIP

Dear *(name):*

At last, the Marketing Club opened the envelope and announced you as the winner. Congratulations on your splendid achievement in winning this year's Silver Circle Award. The honor marks a lifetime of service to both advertising and the community.

I was still a toddler when you started in the business, but that enabled me to learn from your lessons, follow in the path you set, and bask in your legend. I cannot say that I knew you when, but I am glad I know you now.

Again, congratulations. I cannot think of a more worthy recipient.

Sincerely,

Signature

Name
Title

17d. Congratulations—New Baby

(Name):

You will not believe the fun you're missing here. The work is piling up, the phones are ringing off the hook, Mrs. *(name)* is in a snit, the boys in shipping have decided they are not doing anything today because the All-Star Game has gone into extra innings ...

But then, you just had a baby! And while our world is tumbling around and splitting apart at the seams, you have a pair of bright blue eyes staring up from a rosy pink face in wonder at the new world stretching around her. And laughing. And crying. And cooing. And giggling.

And right now none of us could think of any other place we would rather be than in your shoes. Congratulations from all of us. Enjoy your bundle of joy for as long as you can.

Signatures

17e. CONGRATULATIONS—BIRTHDAY

Date

Name/Title
Business/Organization Name
Address
City, State ZIP

Dear *(name)*:

Let me take this opportunity to wish you the very happiest of birthdays, Mr.
(Name). I have long been an admirer of your style and grace, and I am glad to be
your friend. You are an example to us all.

Thank you for your leadership of this fine firm. I hope your special day is a most
enjoyable one.

Sincerely,

Signature

Name
Title

17f. Congratulations—Anniversary [Business]

Date

Name/Title
Business/Organization Name
Address
City, State ZIP

Dear *(name):*

Congratulations on the 10-year anniversary of *(name of company).* Your service to the city's small businesses is without comparison, and we are pleased that by helping others prosper, you also have made your mark.

Ten years ago, the company was a mere idea of *(name of founder),* who came from a small firm where a little capital, a little consulting, and a lot of hard work can make a big difference. By starting *(name of company), (name of founder)* turned that belief into a commitment, and that commitment into a successful business.

Business in Central City is prospering, and *(name of company)* has played an important role in making that happen. Again, congratulations on ten years of service, and thank you for your excellent work.

Best regards,

Signature

Name
Title

17g. CONGRATULATIONS—CIVIC ACHIEVEMENT

Date

Name/Title
Business/Organization Name
Address
City, State ZIP

Dear *(name)*:

The United Way is proud of its long line of corporate supporters and the generous work they do in soliciting donations and providing services to the community's needy and underprivileged. This year we have broken all records in terms of corporate contributions, and we are proud to say that *(name of company)*'s contribution was among the most significant.

Some companies make their mark in the community by erecting statues or funding buildings they then put their name on. We are pleased that *(name of company)* has chosen to make its contribution in a meaningful way, spending money and devoting effort where it is really needed—helping the less fortunate among us.

A child's smile, not a marble statue, is your reward. We are glad to see that, year after year, that appears to be enough.

Best regards,

Signature

Name
Title

17h. Congratulations—Retirement

Date

Name/Title
Business/Organization name
Address
City, State ZIP

Dear *(name)*:

Can you still see the day you powered up that first room-size Univac "computer," with its hoses and tubes? It hummed like a son-of-a-gun, but it got the job done in its own slow way.

Today's computers process data at lightening speed, and that is how the time seems to have gone since you entered the business. Now you face retirement and a whole new chapter in your life. We want to thank you for all you have given us and wish you well on your journey.

In our estimation, there will never be another computer quite like the old Univac. And there never will be another boss quite like you. Hope your retirement is happy and the rest of your life prosperous and fulfilling.

Best wishes,

Signature

Name

17i. CONGRATULATIONS—RESPONSE

Date

Name/Title
Business/Organization Name
Address
City, State ZIP

Dear *(name)*:

Thank you so much for your kind note. Sometimes things turn out better than you would ever expect them to, and I believe that is what happened to me. I felt honored to win the award, and I appreciate your kind words of congratulations.

The real honor, however, comes from what the project meant to the hundreds of people who benefited from it. Easing their struggle is my real reward. The rest is all boilerplate.

The award does look nice on the mantel, though. Thanks again for writing.

Sincerely,

Signature

Name
Title

18a. Credit and Collections—Requesting Payment

Date

Name/Title
Business/Organization Name
Address
City, State ZIP

Dear *(name)*:

Our Accounting Department has informed us that the invoice for the shipment of office furniture dated January 14 is more than sixty days past due. They have asked me as the salesman of record to contact you regarding payment.

Since we have always had a good relationship and your past invoices have always been paid promptly within thirty days, we assume that this particular invoice has been mislaid or that there is some other simple explanation. I have assured Accounting that there will be no trouble in this case and that they can expect your check soon.

I would appreciate your immediate attention to this matter and the receipt of your payment within the next two weeks. If there are circumstances that will cause further delays, please contact me immediately, and I will be happy to do whatever I can to help you to solve this problem.

We appreciate your continued business. Please call if you have any questions.

Best wishes,

Signature

Name
Title

18b. CREDIT AND COLLECTIONS—PROMISING PAYMENT

Date

Name/Title
Business/Organization Name
Address
City, State ZIP

Dear *(name):*

We have received your recent inquiry and are fully aware that we are sixty days in arrears. We appreciate your patience and your willingness to help us resolve this situation.

The current economy has had a negative effect on business growth. That, along with some short-term notes coming due, has caused a temporary cash flow crunch for our firm. We look forward to that flow being restored within the next two to three months as the notes are satisfied and some new products enter the market.

Our outstanding invoice totals $3,760. Enclosed please find a check for $1,000 to help satisfy that debt. We anticipate paying you an additional $1,000 each month for two months, and the balance of $760 by mid-July.

Again, we appreciate your patience and flexibility and look forward to our continued relationship.

Sincerely,

Signature

Name
Title

18c. Credit and Collections—Investigation

Date

Name/Title
Business/Organization Name
Address
City, State ZIP

Dear *(name):*

Last March, we sent you a notice that your invoice for the shipment of office furniture dated January 14 was more than sixty days past due. Your response of March
21 indicated minor cash flow problems. The letter was accompanied by a check for
$1,000 and an anticipated payment schedule designed to satisfy the remaining debt
of $2,760 by mid-July.

As of August 15, we had received neither additional payments nor explanations for
the further delay. Attempts to contact you by telephone failed and, in making our
most recent call, we were informed that your line had been disconnected.

Within five days of this letter we will be turning this matter over to our collections
bureau, which will launch a formal investigation of this case and, if necessary, institute legal proceedings. If the debt is satisfied prior to that date, we will take no further action.

Please notify us immediately to help all of us avoid this embarrassing and costly
procedure.

Very truly yours,

Signature

Name
Title

18d. CREDIT AND COLLECTIONS—OFFER OF CREDIT

Date

Name/Title
Business/Organization Name
Address
City, State ZIP

Dear *(name):*

In today's uncertain economy, there simply are too many risks.

That goes for our customers, too. We selectively choose those with whom we prefer to do business and those to whom we extend credit. It is a precautionary measure that helps keep service costs down, allowing us to offer the most competitive rates possible to those we serve.

After a close review of your credit history, we are pleased to offer your company a full line of credit toward purchases made from our business. Please fill out the attached application, which will allow us to set up your account.

Welcome to our customer family. We look forward to doing more business with you.

Sincerely,

Signature

Name
Title

18e. CREDIT AND COLLECTIONS—REFUSING CREDIT

Date

Name/Title
Business/Organization Name
Address
City, State ZIP

Dear *(name)*:

Thank you for your recent offer of credit. We have managed to keep our credit history clean by taking great care as to how we use that credit and with whom we do business. While we appreciate your generous offer, we respectfully decline your extension of credit.

Your firm seems like a fine one, and your offer certainly is generous. But too many companies we know have gotten in over their heads and are now credit-poor. We would like to maintain our high rating, and choose not to accept your line of credit.

Sincerely,

Signature

Name
Title

18f. CREDIT AND COLLECTIONS—CANCELLING CREDIT

Date

Name/Title
Business/Organization Name
Address
City, State ZIP

Dear *(name)*:

We regret to inform you that we are forced to cancel both personal and corporate lines of credit to Windsong Industries. As of October 1, your firm was $48,385 in arrears. While we applaud the intent of your business, we believe that management has failed to provide adequate expense control, given your status as a start-up business.

(Name), an attorney with the firm *(name of firm),* will be in contact shortly about arranging repayment of both personal and corporate debt. We believe there are ways
to make Windsong Industries more operationally efficient and satisfy the debt more quickly. With any luck, we will also have you up and offering alternative energy to more area residents shortly.

Please have your financial records in order when the bank representative calls. We look forward to resolving this matter to our mutual satisfaction.

Very truly yours,

Signature

Name
Title

18g. CREDIT AND COLLECTIONS—CASUAL REMINDER

Date

Name/Title
Business/Organization Name
Address
City, State ZIP

Dear *(name)*:

Just a reminder that your account at Travis Hardware now totals $188.55. We would appreciate payment of this amount so that we can clear the books for the month of June. If you have already sent a check, please accept our thanks for settling the balance.

Sincerely,

Signature

Name
Title

18h. CREDIT AND COLLECTIONS—STRONGER REMINDER

Date

Name/Title
Business/Organization Name
Address
City, State ZIP

Dear *(name)*:

To date we have not received your payment of $188.55 due to Travis Hardware. Will you please put your check in the enclosed envelope and mail it immediately? Thank you.

Sincerely,

Signature

Name
Title

18i. CREDIT AND COLLECTIONS—DEMAND FOR PAYMENT

Date

Name/Title
Business/Organization Name
Address
City, State ZIP

Dear *(name):*

Your account at Travis Hardware in the amount of $188.55 is 120 days delinquent. No further credit will be extended to you until this amount has been satisfied.

We demand immediate payment or a suitable explanation as to why we will not receive such payment. Please return your payment in the enclosed self-addressed stamped envelope.

Your failure to respond to this notice will force us to contact our attorney and institute collection procedures.

Sincerely,

Signature

Name
Title

19a. DISMISSALS—LAYOFFS [GENERIC]

Date

Name/Title
Business/Organization name
Address
City, State ZIP

Dear *(name):*

It is no secret from any of our employees that *(name of company)* is facing a major downturn in the *(name of industry)* market. This has forced our firm to make several major cost-cutting moves. We are sorry to inform you that, as of *(date)*, your position has been *(permanently/temporarily)* eliminated.

Please recognize that this is no reflection on your performance. We appreciate the years you have served *(shortened name of company)* and the contributions you have made. Unfortunately, reduced market demand for products manufactured in your area have forced the closure and/or consolidation of several production facilities. We no longer need as many workers, and we are forced to eliminate your position.

We sympathize and understand the problems unemployment poses for you and your family, and our human resources department will do everything possible to assist in outplacement services. This is an unfortunate time for all concerned. Let's hope both the economy and our industry will make a fast recovery.

Sincerely,

Signature

Name
Title

19b. Dismissals—Layoffs (Seasonal)

Date

Name/Title
Business/Organization Name
Address
City, State ZIP

Dear *(name):*

As fall draws to a close, it is time once again to evaluate the workforce we will need to get us through until spring. As you may have expected, the call for concrete finishers in our area during the winter months is limited to nonexistent. This is official notification that you will be laid off until March 1 or later, depending both on the weather and on market demand for services.

This is standard operating procedure for the construction industry and is no reflection either on you or on your past performance. We have always appreciated the hard work and initiative you have shown at *(name of company)*, and we look forward to working together again in the coming year.

If you need references for seasonal or temporary employment, please feel free to call.

With best wishes,

Signature

Name
Title

19c. DISMISSALS—LAYOFFS [PERMANENT]

Date

Name/Title
Business/Organization Name
Address
City, State ZIP

Dear *(name):*

This letter serves as official notification of the permanent closing of our imaging division and the elimination of all positions in that division. That includes your position as technical manager.

This letter follows the formal and informal discussions with managers and employee groups prior to the announcement of the purchase of our company by Inland Chemical. As a condition of that purchase, current management agreed to divest its less profitable divisions, one of which was the imaging division. We are sorry that the move resulted in job losses for you and so many loyal and valuable employees.

Within sixty days of Inland Chemical's purchase and assumption of our firm, they will announce a new corporate structure. Past employees will be given preferential treatment in applying for any positions for which they may qualify. We would encourage you to consider returning to the firm in another capacity.

In the interim, please accept our sincerest regrets over this necessary move, and accept our best wishes for future success.

Sincerely,

Signature

Name
Title

19d. Dismissals—Firing (Warning)

Date

Name/Title
Business/Organization Name
Address
City, State ZIP

Dear *(name)*:

Employee discipline is a difficult task, but after several verbal warnings regarding *(name of offence)*, we are forced to warn you in writing, as per state law, of possible termination.

According to the record in your personnel file, you did on *(date/dates)* *(describe the offense as it relates to violation of company policies)*. These offenses were brought to your attention verbally on *(date/dates)* by *(name of supervisor and/or witnesses)*.

Your actions are in clear violation of *(policy)* and will not be tolerated. The above-mentioned instances constitute the necessary verbal warnings. This will be your one and only written warning. Any further violation of these policies will result in immediate termination.

Sincerely,

Signature

Name
Title

19e. DISMISSALS—FIRING [FINAL]

Date

Name/Title
Business/Organization Name
Address
City, State ZIP

Dear *(name):*

After considerable review and several warnings, it has become necessary to termi-
nate your position as *(name of position)* for *(name of firm)*. As of today, you no
longer will be an employee here.

A review of our records shows that your performance as ranked by your supervisor
has been substandard and that your attitude toward your job, your coworkers, and
this firm has been negative. Repeated verbal and written warnings have failed to
elicit any improvement in either performance or attitude. Your continued employment threatens the productivity and morale of the department and of the firm.

We are sorry that this step had to be taken, but, considering the circumstances, there
were no other alternatives. Consider today your last day at *(name of firm)*. Please
collect all personal belongings and vacate the building by 4 p.m.

Sincerely,

Signature

Name
Title

20a. EMPLOYMENT OFFERS [GENERIC]   Note: See letter 23d for an alternative version of a job offer.

Date

Name/Title
Business/Organization Name
Address
City, State ZIP

Dear *(name):*

It is our pleasure to extend to you the position of *(name of position)* with *(name of company)*. The position reports to *(name and title of supervisor)* in the *(name of department or division)*.

Your position responsibilities will include *(list of responsibilities, including number and nature of employees supervised)*. In addition, *(list of other responsibilities)* will be required.

Your compensation has been set at *(amount)*, with full benefits as outlined in the employee handbook. In addition, *(list additional perks, such as club memberships, company car, and other benefits)*. Your first day of work will be *(date)*.

We hope you will accept this offer and we look forward to welcoming you to what we hope will be a rewarding career with *(name of company)*.

Kindest regards,

Signature

Name
Title

20b. Employment Offers—Acceptance

Date

Name/Title
Business/Organization Name
Address
City, State ZIP

Dear (name):

Thank you for your generous offer. I am pleased to accept the job of *(title of position)*.

Project duties at my current position can be wrapped up in *(number of days)*, at which time I can make the move to *(name of new company)*. My current employer already has been informed that I have been looking, and it remains now only for me to give him the date of my departure.

Thank you for this wonderful opportunity. I look forward to all the challenges Whalen will throw my way, and to making a positive contribution to the firm.

Sincerely,

Signature

Name

20c. Employment Offers—Rejection by Candidate

Date

Name/Title
Business/Organization Name
Address
City, State ZIP

Dear *(name)*:

Thank you for your offer, but I must decline the position of office manager for Nip 'n' Tuck Stitchery.

Your offer is generous, but my personal life has taken a turn that would make my acceptance of the position problematic right now. You need an active, dynamic, and effective manager. But until my personal issues have been resolved, I do not believe I can give the position the attention it deserves.

Please accept my sincerest regrets, and thanks again for your offer.

Best regards,

Signature

Name

20d. EMPLOYMENT OFFERS—REJECTION BY EMPLOYER [GENERIC]

Date

Name/Title
Business/Organization Name
Address
City, State ZIP

Dear *(name)*:

Thank you for your interest in the *(name of position)* position we recently advertised. We heard from many potential candidates, and we were impressed with your qualifications.

Though it was a difficult choice, we found another candidate we feel was even more qualified for the position and the company. Therefore, we are sorry to inform you that we cannot offer you the job.

Other positions do come along, one of which may be suited to your qualifications. We have taken the liberty of retaining your application in our files in hopes of finding a good match. In the meantime, we wish you the best of luck in your career search, and thanks again for your interest in our firm.

Sincerely,

Signature

Name
Title

21a. EXPENSES—QUESTIONING

MEMORANDUM

TO: VP Sales
FROM: Accounting Supervisor
DATE:
SUBJECT: Travel Expenses

In reviewing your recent travel expense vouchers, we have noted a continual increase in the number and duration of telephone calls made from your hotel room during business trips. This situation reached alarming levels during your recent trip to New York City, where your calls during a three-day stay at the Hilton totaled $91.40.

We appreciate the need for employees to call home and perhaps make other personal calls while away on business, but company policy limits those calls to two per day totaling no more than five minutes in length each. We realize extenuating circumstances may occasionally necessitate longer calls, and have tried to be lenient about these. Your records over the past indicate an increasing violation of that policy, and the current expense level is completely unacceptable.

Please explain in writing the nature and recipients of those calls in question, or enclose a check made out to the company in the amount of $91.40. We are unable to process your expense reimbursement until this request has been satisfied.

Thank you for your prompt attention in this matter.

21b. EXPENSES—RESPONSE TO REQUESTS

MEMORANDUM

TO: Accounting Supervisor
FROM: VP Sales
DATE:
SUBJECT: Expenses Explanation

Thanks for noticing the growing number and cost of phone calls. While I offer no excuse for violating policy, I do have an explanation I think may bear some weight on your judgment.

My wife has suffered several severe health problems for the past four years, and she had a recurrence of a muscle problem while I was recently out of town. This resulted in several calls home to keep up with the situation until I returned. I have explained this to my supervisor, and he agrees with the necessity of the calls.

I have no wish to violate company policy, but you can see these were unusual circumstances, and I trust this explanation will relieve me of having to reimburse the company for the charges on these calls. I know my supervisor agrees with this.

21c. Expenses—Accepting Explanations

M E M O R A N D U M

TO: VP Sales
FROM: Accounting Supervisor
DATE:
SUBJECT: Travel Expense Update

I shared your note with *(Name)*, and he and I both sympathize with your situation. The amount in question is large, but your situation is a serious one and we don't want to make it any worse. We will waive repayment of the $91.40 in telephone bills.

We hope your wife's health improves and suggest that your business travel be scaled back until that happens.

21d. Expenses—Rejecting Explanations

M E M O R A N D U M

TO: VP Sales
FROM: Accounting Supervisor
DATE:
SUBJECT: Travel Expense Update

We appreciate your timely response, and sympathize with your wife's illness and the difficulties and discomfort it must cause. However, company policy has clear limits on the number and amount of calls permissible while traveling on business, and your recent bill exceeds them. Were this a one-time incident, we would be inclined to overlook them. But telephone charges for the past nine trips total more than $650, an amount far beyond that we consider permissible.

Given your situation, we will accept $45—less than half the $91.40 you owe for this current trip. But in the future, all telephone calls made during business travel may not be charged to the room and must be paid for through your own personal telephone calling card.

We also suggest you speak to your supervisor about a realignment of duties. Given your current home situation, it seems necessary for you to curtail your travel on company business.

22a. Goodwill—Donations (Giving)

Date

Name/Title
Business/Organization Name
Address
City, State ZIP

Dear *(name)*:

We are familiar with all the good work Operation Wheatstraw has done over the past six decades, and we are excited by the promise of the Global Villages campaign. Please accept our check for $3,000 in support of your effort.

Feel free to apply it to three months' worth of support for one village, or one month each for three villages. What's important to us is that it be used in the best way possible to help the greatest number of people. And the quicker the better.

Good luck in your fundraising and continued success in your humanitarian mission.

Best regards,

Signature

Name
Title

22b. Goodwill—Donations (Refusing)

Date

Name/Title
Business/Organization Name
Address
City, State ZIP

Dear (name):

We received your letter requesting donations for your new Global Villages project. While we applaud your effort and recognize that we have supported Operation Wheatstraw in the past, we must respectfully decline participation at this time.

A combination of limited financial growth and restructured corporate policies have reduced all contribution levels and limited our giving to local charities only. As much as we would like to support your efforts, company policy prohibits international giving.

Please accept our sincere regrets. Best of luck in your new efforts.

Kindest regards,

Signature

Name
Title

22c. Goodwill—Donations [Accepting]

Date

Name/Title
Business/Organization Name
Address
City, State ZIP

Dear *(name):*

The directors of Operation Wheatstraw sincerely thank you for your generous contribution to our new Global Villages project. We will use your contribution of $3,000 to provide a village near Aruc, Uganda, with a new septic system, water purification treatment, grain and vegetables, and lessons in new agricultural methods.

Operation Wheatstraw, and the residents of Uganda, thank you again for your generous support.

With warm regards,

Signature

Name
Title

22d. Goodwill—Recognition of Service (Generic)

Date

Name/Title
Business/Organization Name
Address
City, State ZIP

Dear *(name):*

The theme song for many companies might be, "Hey, what's in it for me?" But that is a song we will never find you singing.

Over the past year, your efforts on behalf of *(name of charity or cause)* have been exceeded only by the commitment and joy you bring to your service. Many people give, and some give more generously than others. But few bring the energy to their contribution that you do. That, in itself, is something no amount of money could buy.

We wish we could compensate you adequately for all the service you have given us, but we know we never will. We can only express our appreciation for all you have done and on behalf of all those you have served. Please know that you have made a big difference in the lives of many people.

Thanks again. Few could match your contribution to our cause.

Best regards,

Signature

Name
Title

22e. Goodwill—Job Well Done (Generic)

Date

Name/Title
Business/Organization Name
Address
City, State ZIP

Dear *(name):*

When we first were told about *(name of firm)*'s attempt to *(name of task or project)*, we were skeptical and even critical. When you joined the team, we knew little about your background and less about your ability. Frankly, we had little faith that the task could be completed as described.

You changed our thinking on that. Through your diligence, hard work, and consummate skill, you demonstrated a new way of approaching *(generic identification of task)* that we had not considered. What's more, you made it work with less demand on resources than we ever would have imagined possible.

(Name of firm) has our renewed faith, especially when it comes to *(generic identification of project)*. And you have our deepest gratitude for a job exceptionally well done. They have a wellspring of talent in you, and we will encourage them to put you to work on our behalf whenever and wherever possible.

Best regards,

Signature

Name
Title

22f. Goodwill—Offering Support During Personal Crisis (Generic)

Date

Name/Title
Business/Organization Name
Address
City, State ZIP

Dear *(name):*

In times like these, we all need a friend, a confidant, or someone we can rely on to help us through a crisis. I just wanted you to know that you have got such a person in me.

We have had the opportunity to work together, share responsibilities, and face challenges. I have always admired your strength and resiliency in dealing with problems, and always thought that, in a crisis, I would like to react the way you would in helping to solve the problem. Now is my chance, and I want you to know that you can count on me.

You know the number. Call if you want to talk. I am ready to lend a hand or an ear when you need it. That, after all, is what friends are for.

Best regards,

Signature

Name

22g. Goodwill—Thanks for the Support [Generic]

Date

Name/Title
Business/Organization Name
Address
City, State ZIP

Dear *(name):*

Given the looks on those directors' faces, I though it would be light-years before they would ever approve a notion like *(name of project).* I was pleased when I got the thumbs-up all around, but not shocked. I knew when you spoke out on my behalf that the project was likely to fly.

We have given each other support before, but never under such extraordinary circumstances. That means a lot to me, and it will have a major impact on the success of this project. A lot of us will have a lot to thank you for down the road, but let me be the first.

Thanks very much. You have been more help than you will ever know.

Sincerely,

Signature

Name

23a. HIRING—RECEIPT OF RESUME (GENERIC)

Date

Name/Title
Business/Organization Name
Address
City, State ZIP

Dear *(name)*:

This letter acknowledges receipt of your resume in application for the position of *(name of position)*. We appreciate your interest and have passed your letter on to the appropriate department head.

Resumes will be screened during the next two weeks, with preliminary candidate selections due to be made by *(date)*. At that time, we will telephone candidates we wish to interview and schedule meetings.

The position has elicited a strong response; thus we cannot answer telephone inquiries about either the position itself or the progress in reviewing your application. Please be patient with us, and we will do all we can to keep you informed.

Thanks you again for your interest in *(name of company)*. We will be in contact with you soon.

Sincerely,

Signature

Name
Title

23b. HIRING—SCHEDULING AN INTERVIEW (GENERIC)

Date

Name/Title
Business/Organization Name
Address
City, State ZIP

Dear *(name):*

We appreciate your interest in and enthusiasm for the position of *(name of position)* here at *(name of company)*. Among the dozens of resumes we received, yours was among the most impressive. We look forward to meeting you and discussing how you may be able to help our firm.

We have scheduled your interview for *(date and time)*. Enclosed is a small map and parking sticker for your use when you visit us. Please park only in the orange "Visitor" section, and place the sticker on your left rear window.

We are looking forward to your interview with us and hope the event is beneficial both for you and for *(short name of company)*.

Sincerely,

Signature

Name
Title

23c. Hiring—Thank You for Interview [Generic]

Date

Name/Title
Business/Organization Name
Address
City, State ZIP

Dear *(name):*

Thank you very much for taking the time to explain the opportunities *(name of company)* and the *(name of position)* position have to offer. It is clear to me now why you are considered the industry leader, and I hope I can help you maintain and increase your competitive edge.

They say the right job not only sounds right, but also feels right. Throughout my career, no position match has felt quite as right as this. I hope you think so, too, and that I have the opportunity to show you what I can do to help you achieve your corporate goals.

Sincerely,

Signature

Name

23d. HIRING—JOB OFFER (GENERIC)   Note: See letter 20a for an alternative version of a job offer.

Date

Name/Title
Business/Organization Name
Address
City, State ZIP

Dear *(name)*:

It is our pleasure to offer you the position of *(name of position)* with *(name of company)*. This offer confirms our verbal offer of *(date)*.

The compensation for this position is *(rate of pay)* and includes *(list of perks)*, all of which our human resources department will explain in detail. As per our mutual agreement, you will begin work on *(date)*.

We look forward to having you on our staff. Your credentials, experience, and attitude all complement our organizational goals. We believe this to be an excellent opportunity both for you and for *(name of company)* to show what we can do.

Congratulations. We look forward to seeing you on *(date)*.

Best regards,

Signature

Name
Title

23e. HIRING—REFUSING A CANDIDATE (GENERIC)

Date

Name/Title
Business/Organization Name
Address
City, State ZIP

Dear *(name)*:

Thank you for your interest in the *(name of position)* position at *(name of company)*. The opening generated a large number of responses, making our decision very difficult.

You have excellent credentials and generated strong interest among our screening committee members. Unfortunately, another candidate proved to be a closer match, and we have offered the position to that person and she has accepted.

We will keep your resume on file in case a similar opportunity should arise. In the meantime, thank you again for your interest, and good luck in your search.

Sincerely,

Signature

Name
Title

24a. HOLIDAY GREETINGS (GENERIC)

Date

Name/Title
Business/Organization Name
Address
City, State ZIP

Dear *(name)*:

It's the time when all of us look forward to prospects and plans for the new year. In this moment of reflection, all of us at *(name of sender's company)* would like to wish all of you at *(name of receiver's company)* the best of holiday greetings.

We've had several opportunities to work together this past year, fulfilling our mutual goals and realizing both personal and professional successes. We look forward to a continuing prosperous relationship with new opportunities for cooperation.

All the best for the new year and for the years to come.

Sincerely,

Signature

Name
Title

24b. HOLIDAY GREETINGS—EXTERNAL (PROFESSIONAL)

Date

Name/Title
Business/Organization Name
Address
City, State ZIP

Dear *(name):*

We'd like to take this opportunity to send our best wishes for a joyous holiday season. My colleagues and I have enjoyed continued success this past year, part of it due to your contributions and assistance. We sincerely hope you have also enjoyed a prosperous year and that the one coming up will be even better.

Please share our best wishes with your employees. And to you and your family, happy holidays!

Warm regards,

Signature

Name
Title

24c. HOLIDAY GREETINGS—EXTERNAL (PERSONAL)

Date

Name/Title
Business/Organization Name
Address
City, State ZIP

Dear *(name):*

This is a time of year when we count our blessings and share good wishes with those who mean something to us throughout the year and, if we're lucky, through-out our lives. Few fit this description as well as you, and if I haven't said it recently, I want to take this seasonal opportunity to wish you the very best.

We've come a long way, and the road has not always been smooth. We have shared both successes and disappointments and have had the opportunity to laugh and to worry together. Those kinds of experiences make deep impressions on a person, and reflecting back during this holiday season brings them to mind.

If I can offer you but one gift this year, let that gift be one of laughter and continued friendship, of success and joy, and of days filled with sunshine and the wisdom to appreciate them.

Happy holidays,

Signature

Name

24d. HOLIDAY GREETINGS—INTERNAL

Date

TO ALL PERSONNEL:

In this season of thanksgiving, *(name of company)* stops and takes stock of the work it has done and the service it has rendered to its customers. In so uncertain an economy, we are fortunate to have found as much loyalty and patronage as we have in the *(name of industry)* market.

The management team knows that such things don't occur in a vacuum, and that, with rare exceptions, they have done no more to influence customer satisfaction than to serve as guides along the road. Our success rests in the hands of people like you all, who directly serve our customers through development, production, sales, and fulfillment, and your work distinguishes us from our competition. People like you and the man or woman working next to you make all the difference.

We deeply appreciate your efforts throughout the year, and wish you and yours the most joyous of holiday seasons.

24e. HOLIDAY GREETINGS—INTERNAL [PERSONAL]

Date:

(Name of recipient):

Business has been good for us the last few months, and shows all the signs of getting even better. Part of that has to do with the improving financial situation. But the biggest satisfaction I get from coming in here every day is being able to work with you on all our different projects, large or small.

Thanks for being a good friend, an able coworker, and one of the *(funniest or nicest or most considerate)* people I have had the pleasure to know. I hope your holidays are happy ones. No one I know deserves it more.

Signature

Name

25a. INFORMATION—REQUESTING (GENERIC)

Date

Name/Title
Business/Organization Name
Address
City, State ZIP

Dear *(name)*:

We read with interest your *(article/comments)* on *(subject)* in *(source of comments)*. No matter which side of the argument one is on, there is something to be gained from the things you said.

We would like *(a copy of / further information about) (subject)*. *(**Optional:** Include statement about the information's intended use.)* Please send the information to us at the following address:

>   Name/title
>   Address/P.O. Box
>   City, State ZIP

Thank you for your assistance. We look forward to reading more of your comments and to the opportunity to take advantage of your expertise.

Best regards,

Signature

Name
Title

25b. INFORMATION—REQUESTING (FROM CLIENT OR CUSTOMER)

Date

Name/Title
Business/Organization Name
Address
City, State ZIP

Dear *(name):*

We received your claim for damages to your car on *(date)*. In your claim, you allege that a group of youths charged your car from a street corner and threw bottles, rocks, and other debris, resulting in the damage to your vehicle for which you have made the claim. However, our adjuster claims that the dents, scrapes, and broken glass more closely resemble the type of accident that occurs when a vehicle strikes or sideswipes a tree, structure, or other vehicle. The flecks of red paint in your vehicle's blue paint help support this argument.

For us to further consider your claim, we need to know more of the particulars of the incident you describe: what time it occurred, how many youths were involved, and the nature of the activity that both preceded and followed the incident. We will also need a completed police report on the incident before we can proceed.

Thank you for your assistance in this matter.

Sincerely,

Signature

Name
Title

25c. Information—Requesting (From Other Source)

Date

Name/Title
Business/Organization Name
Address
City, State ZIP

Dear *(name):*

In the March issue of *Scientific American*, in the article, "A New Look at Sleep Disorders," you refer to a cure involving herbal teas developed by Dr. Rajiv Pradeep. The teas are mixed to produce a nonnarcotic sedative said to work in 70 percent of all cases.

I would be very interested in finding out more about this cure, and about Dr. Pradeep. Please forward any additional information you may have, or an address where I may contact Dr. Pradeep.

Thank you for your assistance. I enjoy your publication very much.

Sincerely,

Signature

Name

25d. Information—Providing

Date

Name/Title
Business/Organization Name
Address
City, State ZIP

Dear *(name):*

Thank you for your recent inquiry. Enclosed you will find the information requested on *(subject)* from *(source of material).*

We have received numerous requests for this information, which has led us to explore other facets of *(subject)* and related topics. If you would like further information as we find it, please return the enclosed postcard with your name and address written on the back. We will keep you on our mailing list for future information.

Thanks for your interest and thanks for reading!

Best regards,

Signature

Name
Title

25e. INFORMATION—PROVIDING (TO CLIENT OR CUSTOMER)

Date

Name/Title
Business/Organization Name
Address
City, State ZIP

Dear *(name):*

In response to your request, we have enclosed more information on our supplemental insurance policy. This information describes insurance that provides health coverage over and above your employer and personal policies. It does not provide death, dismemberment, or disability benefits.

In this world of high-cost health care, supplemental health benefits have enabled thousands of Americans to live more comfortable and confident lives, knowing that they can meet unanticipated health-care costs. It is a form of financial security we highly recommend.

You will soon hear from one of our representatives who will tell you more and answer any questions you might have.

Sincere regards,

Signature

Name
Title

25f. INFORMATION—REFUSING [GENERIC]

Date

Name/Title
Business/Organization Name
Address
City, State ZIP

Dear *(name):*

(Name/title or *department)* has received and reviewed your request for information. We are sorry to report that, because of *(reason)*, we are unable to honor your request.

*(**Optional:** Give rationale for refusing request. Go into whatever detail may be appropriate.)*

We thank you for your interest and regret that we are unable to be of more service.

Sincerely,

Signature

Name
Title

25g. INFORMATION—REFUSING [A CLIENT OR CUSTOMER]

Date

Name/Title
Business/Organization Name
Address
City, State ZIP

Dear *(name):*

We have received your request for more information regarding access to specific procedures regarding bank overdrafts in general, and your account information in particular. A printout of your recent activity is enclosed.

Unfortunately, beyond general procedures, company policy prohibits us from providing more detailed information. This is considered strategic information and may not be revealed except to the bank's executives.

We are sorry we could not be more helpful. If you would like to pursue the matter further, please contact *(name)*, operations manager. If you have any specific requests regarding other aspects of operations, you may also contact *(name)*.

Thank you for your inquiry and continued patronage.

With best wishes,

Signature

Name

26a. Inquiry—Generic

Date

Name/Title
Business/Organization Name
Address
City, State ZIP

Dear *(name):*

We know your firm to be one of the top *(experts on/manufacturers of) (subject of inquiry)* in the country. We plan some significant applications and uses of *(subject)* and would appreciate more detailed knowledge. Can you provide us with that knowledge? We would welcome any recommendations of articles, books, or experts that we could consult.

We will be in touch by telephone within a month, hoping that that will give you enough time to respond to our inquiry. We appreciate any help you can give us.

Best regards,

Signature

Name
Title

26b. Inquiry—Item

Date

Name/Title
Business/Organization Name
Address
City, State ZIP

Dear *(name):*

Fellow amateur antiquers have been excited over my recent find at the Springfield Antique Mall. I have uncovered what looks to be a complete set of Depression glass, including place settings for eight, water glasses and pitcher, sugar bowl and creamer, and a set of dessert bowls. All items are done in a rust brown, rather than the traditional pink or green we are used to seeing.

I have looked through several antique glass catalogues and have consulted several other dealers, none of whom recognize the color or pattern. I know you have written numerous articles on Depression glass and would appreciate your opinion of my find. I have enclosed a color snapshot of the pitcher and glasses.

Thank you for your assistance.

Sincerely,
Signature
Name

26c. INQUIRY—SUBJECT

Date

Name/Title
Business/Organization Name
Address
City, State ZIP

Dear *(name):*

Alligator husbandry is not something most of us are familiar with, but my husband is pursuing a cram course on the subject. We have inherited several breeding pairs of alligators from my uncle, an alligator farmer, and are intent on breeding them for both hides and meat.

One of the pairs includes a rare albino alligator, and we have not been able to find any information on the genetic likelihood that the animal's albinism will be passed on to future generations. We need to find out if the albinism is transmitted genetically and, if so, how frequently we may expect albino animals. This will help us decide whether to breed this animal.

We have read several of your studies and wonder what you may know about this subject. We appreciate your swift reply.

Best regards,

Signature

Name
Title

26d. INQUIRY—SITUATION

Date

Name/Title
Business/Organization Name
Address
City, State ZIP

Dear *(name)*:

Your advertisement for a nanny in last month's *Domestic Monthly* came to my attention recently, and I wondered if the position was still available.

I have had twelve years of domestic child care experience, including work for several prominent Danish families in Copenhagen. I am experienced in education, music, the arts, and languages. My resume and references are attached.

Your position announcement is old, but I hope the situation is still available. After a brief hiatus, I am eager to get back to caring for little ones, and your position sounds like just the type of situation I would enjoy.

Thank you for consideration. I look forward to your reply.

Sincerely,

Signature

Name

26e. INQUIRY—PERSON

Date

Name/Title
Business/Organization Name
Address
City, State ZIP

Dear *(name):*

In 1985, your firm employed a Mr. *(name)* in the position of chief financial officer. Mr. *(name)* has had both a personal and professional relationship with this office, and we are seeking him to clear up some unfinished business. At one time Mr. *(name)* also listed Mr. *(name)* of your firm as a professional reference. That listing and his past association with your office led us to think you may be able to contact him.

Rest assured that Mr. *(name)* is not in any trouble. When he worked for this company he purchased several shares of stock, then resigned suddenly, leaving the certificates of ownership behind. We have been holding the stock and attempting to locate Mr. *(name)* without success. We thought Mr. *(name)* might like to sell the shares, or at least take possession of the certificates.

Please call and let us know whether you can help us locate Mr. *(Name)*. Thank you for your assistance.

Sincerely,

Signature

Name
Title

27a. INTRODUCTION—GENERIC

Date

Name/Title
Business/Organization Name
Address
City, State ZIP

Dear *(name)*:

These days, many professionals have the training, but few have the drive to apply that training in a way that will make a difference in helping an organization move forward. It is my pleasure to introduce just such a person, *(name)*.

(Describe the individual's background and training as it applies to the professional tasks at hand. Then explain how that background is enhanced by the individual's unique characteristics and ability to help the recipient organization improve its operations/productivity.)

It has been our pleasure to have known and worked with *(name)* for *(length of time)*. *(His/her)* efforts on our behalf have always been exceptional, and the results of those efforts successful. We expect you will have the same experience.

If we can provide further information, please do not hesitate to call.

Best regards,

Signature

Name
Title

27b. INTRODUCTION—OF NEW EMPLOYEE

MEMORANDUM

TO: All Staff
FROM: Vice President/Human Resources
DATE:
SUBJECT: Welcome *(Name)*

After an extensive search, we are pleased to announce that *(name)* has just been named president and CEO by Tirewell's board of directors. *(Name)* comes to us from Running Light Manufacturing, where he served as senior vice president and chief operating officer for the last 12 years. *(Name)* brings with him a wealth of experience and is both well known and respected within our industry.

(Highlight person's achivements in second paragraph.)

(Name) will start May 1. Each department head will have a chance to meet privately with him to share views and concerns, and a general meeting of all staff will be held in the Sourdough Memorial Auditorium on May 21. During those first three weeks, *(name)* also will be meeting with the board of directors and touring our various production facilities. If you see him, please help us make him feel welcome here at Tirewell.

27c. INTRODUCTION—OF AN OUTSIDE FIRM

Date

Name/Title
Business/Organization Name
Address
City, State ZIP

Dear *(name):*

These days, high-tech alternatives abound, and everyone with a personal computer is trying to be the next Bill Gates, writing software that will open the door to the future. This is especially true for the motion picture special effects industry, where simple reshuffling of bits and bytes can morph screen images into pots of gold.

But of all the Spielbergian disciples and would-be wizards, probably the most innovative are the Technocats, three guys who have combined old technologies with new approaches in a way that will make your head spin . . . literally. At least it made our heads spin, and that is why we are delighted to present them to you.

They can introduce themselves by name—we think you will be pleasantly surprised at their secret identities. But suffice it to say that they are very well educated, holding degrees from MIT, Stanford, the University of North Carolina at Chapel Hill, and Cambridge University. They have also worked for some major film directors and producers both here and overseas. Their list of credits, many earned behind the scenes, is as impressive as it is long.

Enclosed you will find a sample reel of their work. We guarantee that you will recognize some of it and be astounded by most of it. And if you are not just dying to call them up when you are done watching, we will not only eat our hats, but also our entire heads . . . and we will have the Technocats send you a video of the event to prove it.

Best regards,

Signature

Name
Title

28a. INVITATION—GENERIC

Date

Name/Title
Business/Organization Name
Address
City, State ZIP

Dear *(name):*

(Name of company) has scheduled a *(gathering/open house)* in honor of *(event or occasion)* on *(date)* at *(time)*. We request the honor of your presence to help us *(celebrate/recognize)* this occasion.

(Name of company) long has been a leader in the field of *(name of industry)*, and we recognize the contributions those outside our own corporate structure have made to our success. You are one such individual, and the board of directors of *(name of company)* would be pleased if you would join them on this important occasion.

Please respond by *(date)*, letting us know if you can attend. We look forward to your participation, and welcome any guest you may bring.

Sincerely,

Signature

Name
Title

28b. Invitation—To Speak (Extending)

Date

Name/Title
Business/Organization Name
Address
City, State ZIP

Dear *(name)*:

The Rotary Club of Cedar Rapids is proud of its members' professional accomplishments, and prouder still of their combined service in the United States armed forces. As Veterans Day approaches, all our thoughts turn to the recent conflicts around the world, and how the American military role has changed in defining peace and protecting democracy. Many of us wonder what may be next for what is still the world's greatest military power, and we're confident that you may be the person to tell us.

Your extensive experience in the Vietnam conflict, the Gulf War, and the humanitarian mission to Somalia, gives you a clearer view of what may lie ahead. We invite you to speak to our luncheon group when it meets this coming Veterans Day at The State House Restaurant.

Our group is composed of community business leaders with a strong interest in public affairs. They have already expressed interest in you as their top luncheon speaker choice, and feel that the Veterans Day meeting would be the perfect venue for your thoughts.

We hope that your calendar is clear and that you will be able to join us for camaraderie and an excellent luncheon before sharing your thoughts. Please contact me by next Thursday with your plans. And thank you for your sincere consideration.

Best regards,

Signature

Name
Title

28c. INVITATION—TO SPEAK [ACCEPTING]

Date

Name/Title
Business/Organization Name
Address
City, State ZIP

Dear *(name):*

Thank you for your recent letter and gracious invitation to the Cedar Rapids Rotary Club. As a matter of fact, my calendar is open on that date, and I would be glad to address so distinguished a group of business leaders, veterans, and patriots.

The one advantage to aging is that it lengthens your perspective and, if you're lucky, gives you a clearer view of the world. I don't know how profound my thoughts may be on the subject you have outlined, but I do have some definite ideas on where we have been and where we may be headed. And I think those views may surprise you and your fellow Rotarians.

My attaché, Lt. Col. Ron Feldman, will be in touch with your office to make further arrangements and provide any additional information you may need. Thank you again for your invitation. I look forward to meeting with you and your group this coming Veterans Day.

God bless America,

Signature

Name
Title

28d. INVITATION—TO SPEAK [DECLINING/REFERRING]

Date

Name/Title
Business/Organization Name
Address
City, State ZIP

Dear *(name):*

Thank you for your gracious invitation to speak to the Rotary Club of Cedar Rapids on Veterans Day. Unfortunately, military business takes me to Geneva, Switzerland, for that entire week. Otherwise, I would have been pleased to accept your invitation.

Since your topic is recent military events, may I take the liberty of suggesting an alternative speaker? Lt. Gen. Francis Xavier Palmieri served beside me during the Persian Gulf conflict and has assisted my efforts in Somalia. A West Point man, Frank is a specialist in military strategy and deployment. He also is currently at work on a project that he is not at liberty to reveal, but that gives him an understanding of possible future trends both profound and disturbing.

My attaché, Lt. Col. Ron Feldman, can make the necessary arrangements to have Frank substitute on my behalf. He will be in touch with your office shortly to help in any way he can. I highly recommend Frank and think you and your fellow Rotarians will find him engaging, informative, and an excellent speaker.

God bless America,

Signature

Name
Title

28e. INVITATION—TO SPEAK [THANK YOU]

Date

Name/Title
Business/Organization Name
Address
City, State ZIP

Dear *(name):*

Our members rarely appreciate a substitute speaker, but in your case they seem to
have made an exception. Evaluations are still coming in, but those we have already
received have cited you as one of the convention's top presenters. Congratulations!

Enclosed please find your honorarium as promised. We would like to book you for
next year, perhaps as part of a tag team with your esteemed cohort. Next year's
event is at the Hilton Hawaiian Village in Honolulu, Hawaii, so we know attendance will be high. We hope the two of you will be able to join us.

We will be sending you further information nearer to the meeting date. Until then,
thank you again for an excellent presentation.

Sincerely,

Signature

Name
Title

28f. INVITATION—TO AN EVENT (EXTENDING)

Date

Name/Title
Business/Organization Name
Address
City, State ZIP

Dear *(name):*

The State Street Emporium is growing in its service to metropolitan Dade County. We have planned a gala celebration and open house to commemorate our success and set our sights on future growth.

Won't you chase away the blues of income tax season and join us Saturday, April 16 for champagne, caviar, and dancing to the music of Jimmy Changa and his Salsa Allstars? The open house will run from 5 p.m. until 10 p.m.

Bring your dancing shoes and your favorite partner. We'll take care of the rest.

Cheers,

Signature

Name
Title

28g. INVITATION—TO AN EVENT (ACCEPTING)

Date

Name/Title
Business/Organization Name
Address
City, State ZIP

Dear *(name):*

Our sales staff is delighted to accept your invitation to State Street Emporium's upcoming open house. We look forward to the entertainment and the chance to socialize with members of your staff.

We are pleased that your store is prospering on so grand a scale. As a long-time supplier, we love to see our customers grow and thrive, because it means more business for all of us.

Thanks again for the invitation. We'll see you on Saturday.

Best regards,

Signature

Name
Title

28h. Invitation—To an Event [Declining, Specific Reason]

Date

Name/Title
Business/Organization Name
Address
City, State ZIP

Dear *(name):*

We received your invitation to State Street Emporium's upcoming open house, but regret that we are unable to attend. It is against our policy to support businesses that indulge in discriminatory practices.

As a social service agency serving a primarily Cuban-American clientele, it has been brought to our attention that, while you gladly take money from the Cuban community, you fail to employ any Cuban staff above the level of janitor. Further, those that do work for you have reported specific instances of discrimination in the areas of promotion, pay raises, and discipline.

Under the circumstances, accepting your invitation would be inappropriate for us.

Sincerely,

Signature

Name
Title

28i. INVITATION—TO PARTICIPATE (EXTENDING)

Date

Name/Title
Business/Organization Name
Address
City, State ZIP

Dear *(name):*

The third annual Coachella Valley Special Olympics committee has set aside the week of May 4–9 to host one of the Inland Empire's most significant fundraising events to benefit the physically and mentally disabled. This time of year dozens of communities host dozens of such events, but you can help make ours very special this year.

We know that as a disabled Vietnam veteran, you have seen more than your share of suffering in service to your country, but we also think you may know a little more of what our Special Olympians may be suffering in terms of social inconvenience and ostracism. That, coupled with physical and administrative experience, makes you a very special contributor. We would like to ask you to participate as an official during this year's games.

There are two dozen positions available, from honorary team coaches, to starters, to judges, to award presenters, all of which we would like to be filled by disabled veterans such as yourself. You have special abilities we would like to tap on behalf of our Olympians. They need someone important to guide them, and we are hoping that someone will be you.

Will you join us to make this a special week for some special people? The attached opportunity form outlines the positions available. We hope you will review it and choose several by the time Games Coordinator Anne Watson calls next week. And we hope you will say yes when she asks for your help.

Thank you for your kind consideration. We hope to see you at the Indio Fairgrounds in May for this year's Special Olympics.

Best regards,

Signature

Name
Title

28j. INVITATION—TO PARTICIPATE (ACCEPTING)

Date

Name/Title
Business/Organization Name
Address
City, State ZIP

Dear *(name):*

Your recent letter took me completely by surprise. I have been lucky to be among the few veterans to have surmounted much of the despair and hate that my disability has caused, but I'm smart enough to know that I haven't done it alone. It took my wife, my children, my friends, my family, and my coworkers to help me. They are all special people to whom I am deeply indebted.

Your Olympians are special people, too, and they also need more than the average share of helping hands. I am happy and honored to pledge my support in making their week an exceptional one.

I have reviewed the opportunity and checked several possible positions in which I may be able to serve. I am looking forward to Ms. Watson's call and to the chance to help these kids excel.

I would guess you won't get this same positive response from all vets. If I can do anything to solicit support and help you overcome obstacles, please feel free to call. In most cases, I speak their language.

Thank you for the invitation. I'm looking forward to helping out.

Sincerely,

Signature

Name

28k. Invitation—To an Event (Declining, Generic)

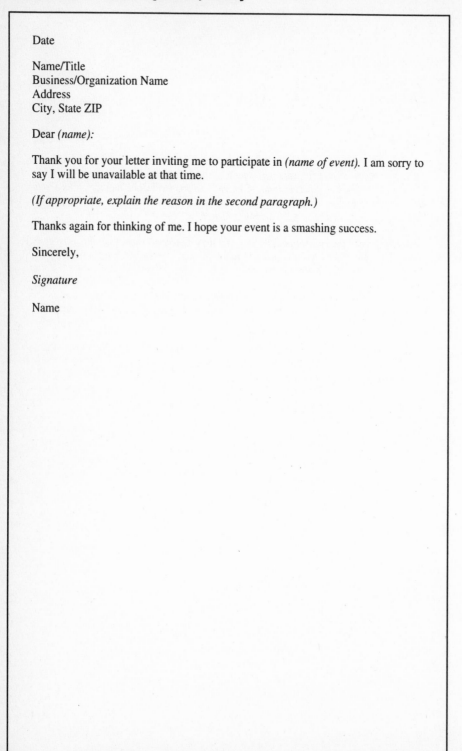

Date

Name/Title
Business/Organization Name
Address
City, State ZIP

Dear *(name):*

Thank you for your letter inviting me to participate in *(name of event).* I am sorry to say I will be unavailable at that time.

(If appropriate, explain the reason in the second paragraph.)

Thanks again for thinking of me. I hope your event is a smashing success.

Sincerely,

Signature

Name

29a. Issues—Managing a Crisis

Date

Name/Title
Business/Organization Name
Address
City, State ZIP

Dear *(name)*:

Color photos have been splashed across the front page of the local newspaper, and last night's news was awash in footage of orange, searing flames. By now, you have heard about the fire that all but destroyed the building housing Heartland Savings & Loan Association. As a depositor, this no doubt has caused you concern. But I am writing you as president of the institution to assure you that your deposited funds are safe and that we are well on the way to recovery.

What you have seen is true; the fire has completely destroyed our physical operation. You no longer will be able to transact business at our Meadowland Road headquarters. But technology has enabled us to save the bulk of our operation, and your files and records are safe in our off-site storage facility. We will be ready to transact business within two days of your receiving this letter.

A temporary facility has been established at 3600 Briarpatch Court, where we will process over-the-counter transactions. If you have a checking account with us, your checks will continue to be accepted and processed through Gordon Trust, our correspondent bank. Your savings, insured by the Federal Deposit Insurance Corp., are available to you any time. They continue to be safe and your account active with us for as long as you so choose.

If you have any specific questions about operations, feel free to call the Heartland Hotline number listed on this letterhead. Attendants are ready to answer questions twenty-four hours a day. We thank you for your patience. A disaster like this is never easy to overcome, but your support makes it that much easier.

Best regards,

Signature

Name
Title

29b. Issues—Encouraging Participation

Date

Name/Title
Business/Organization Name
Address
City, State ZIP

Dear *(name):*

As a member of the Oklahoma City Eagles Club, I only have two words to say to you: Mary Gordon.

Most of you know Mary as the harmless elderly woman who greets us outside each time we come to a meeting at The Exclusive Club. Sometimes Mary is funny, sometimes acerbic, but she always says something memorable. It would not be an Eagles meeting without some comment from Mary.

Mary Gordon also is an alcoholic. What's more, she is homeless, living alternately in a shelter or a cardboard box in an alley down the street from the club. Mary is not an empty face in an anonymous news photo. She is a weekly part of our lives, and she needs our help.

(Name), owner of The Exclusive Club, has begun a Mary Gordon Fund, and we have enlisted the aid of several social service agencies to help us bring Mary in from the cold, treat her alcoholism, and find her a permanent place to live. But we need financial and physical help. If you know of a place where Mary can be put up, no matter how temporary, contact *(name)*. We are asking for a contribution to help Mary. If we each chip in $20, we can start Mary on the road to a new life before it's too late.

We think this is worthwhile doing and hope you will as well. Thanks for your support.

Best wishes,

Signature

Name
Title

29c. Issues—Addressing

Date

Name/Title
Business/Organization Name
Address
City, State ZIP

Dear *(name)*:

We have heard of some wild schemes to raise public funds, Mayor Stockton, but never before have we heard of a $50 parking fee for out-of-town commuters. We think the general public will be as resistant to the idea as we are, and we doubt that you will get the support you need to pass the measure.

Consider the facts: Roughly 40 percent of the city's working population lives outside the city limits. In the case of some companies, that number grows to nearly 80 percent of the workforce. Employers that are unable to ante up for every out-of-towner they have working for them face one more expense in recruiting talent. And enough of these hurdles could send employers looking for cheaper offices in one of the surrounding communities, one that would welcome the business and would not tax commuters.

We urge you to reconsider your plan. It will only drive a bigger wedge between the business community and your office.

Thanks for the consideration. We think this is the best interests of all.

Regards,

Signature

Name
Title

29d. Issues—Addressing a Business Leader

Date

Name/Title
Business/Organization Name
Address
City, State ZIP

Dear *(name)*:

Thank you for your recent letter, but my office respectfully disagrees. A $50 parking assessment for out-of-town residents is, indeed, a good idea, and one that is fair to the resident taxpayers of this city.

Consider the facts: Out-of-town residents who work in the city drive on city streets, enjoy city police and fire protection, walk on city sidewalks, picnic in city parks, and avail themselves of other services—all financially supported by city taxpayers. It is hardly fair for them to get these services free while others carry the financial burden. A commuter tax is one of the fairest ways to get them to "ante up."

Employers may indeed balk at paying the freight. But they should not have to, any more than they should fill the gas tanks, replace the tires, or finance the tune-ups for those who choose to live out of town. These individuals have made that choice, and they should be willing to pay whatever the toll is for the less expensive, more peaceful suburban life.

I would be happy to talk with you further on this, but I have no intention of abandoning my position.

Sincerely,

Signature

Name
Title

29e. Issues—Addressing a Public Forum

Date

Name/Title
Business/Organization name
Address
City, State ZIP

Dear *(name):*

We thank the City Council for agreeing to consider our complaint against operations conducted by the Fordham Rendering Plant just outside the Acorn Heights neighborhood. While we realize that the plant contributes financially to the city, it has become a burden and a hazard for area residents, and we respectfully request that it be denied permission to continue to operate at its current location.

When Fordham opened its doors in 1939, it was located far beyond city limits and away from the general population. It was a major employer, its rendering capabilities were a vital industrial resource for the city, and its presence was beneficial. We realize that this is one of the oldest companies still operating within city limits.

Since Fordham's founding, the city has grown out around it and the market for renderings has all but dried up. Fordham employs one-fifth the employees it did at its height in 1942. Its facilities are old, and its safety standards questionable. The firm has received no fewer than 11 OSHA warnings in the past two years, and its financial value to the community has become negligible.

We urge the City Council to reconsider the business's place in this community and vote to close Fordham down. It has become an eyesore and a public nuisance. And its days of serving the community are long since past.

Sincerely,

Signature

Name
Title

30a. MEETINGS—ANNOUNCING

MEMORANDUM

TO: All Staff
FROM: *(Name)*
DATE:

The Research and Development Division will report its latest findings Friday, April 12, at 8 a.m. in the Norbert Rasmussen Auditorium. All department heads and managers are required to attend.

R&D's findings will form the basis for our new five-year plan. The importance of these issues cannot be underestimated, and senior management does not believe any department heads will be able to draft next year's strategic plan and budget without this information.

If you have an unavoidable conflict, please see Grace Allgood about scheduling a private briefing. Otherwise, we look forward to seeing you on Friday.

31a. ORDER—PLACING

Date

Name/Title
Business/Organization Name
Address
City, State ZIP

Dear (name):

We would like to order two Minolta copiers (Product #36117) as listed in your spring catalogue for $1,832. The copiers should be sent to:

Receiving Dept.
Terrapin Industries
3002 Industrial Dr.
San Rafael, CA 96453
Attn: Sam Johnson

The invoice, with the product shipping date listed, should be sent to:

Accounting Dept.
Attn: Gwen Hadley
ACME Multiglomerate Inc.
13761 Bonny Meadow Rd.
Indianapolis, IN 45398

We would appreciate a timely turnaround on this order. Ship via the normal common carrier your firm uses.

Thank you.

Sincerely,

Signature

Name
Title

31b. ORDER—FILLING

Date

Name/Title
Business/Organization Name
Address
City, State ZIP

Dear *(name):*

We have forwarded the two dozen drums of HyTex industrial cleaner you requested to your warehouse in Bakersfield, CA, for distribution to your other facilities. An invoice for $1,311 plus $69 in delivery charges has been forwarded to your corporate office in Sparks, NV.

According to our records, this shipment is the third and last of the order you placed May 15, for eight dozen drums of HyTex. Please notify us if we are in error in assuming this is the final shipment. We appreciate your business and look forward to serving your industrial cleaning needs again in the future.

Sincerely,

Signature

Name
Title

31c. Order—Delays/Back Order

Date

Name/Title
Business/Organization Name
Address
City, State ZIP

Dear *(name)*:

We received your order for 300 work smocks of varying styles and sizes with the Ford Motor Co. emblem June 13. We are sorry to have to tell you that your shipment will be delayed because of manufacturer error at our supplying plant in Pakistan.

Recent civil unrest has made it sometimes difficult to secure materials from our stitchers and assemblers there. Our overseas supplier tells us that a shortage of raw cotton has added to the problem and that all orders have been delayed two weeks.

We regret any inconvenience this may have caused and look forward to filling your order as soon as the materials arrive. If, after two weeks, the smocks have not yet appeared, we will gladly substitute a higher-grade, more expensive product from our plant in Brazil at no extra charge to you.

We appreciate your patience and value your business. If this solution is not acceptable to you, please call Monty Weber immediately, and we will make whatever arrangements are necessary to satisfy your need. Again, we apologize for the inconvenience.

Sincerely,

Signature

Name
Title

31d. ORDER—DELAY/MORE INFORMATION NEEDED

Date

Name/Title
Business/Organization Name
Address
City, State ZIP

Dear *(name):*

We received your enrollment form and credit card payment for the Management Symposium scheduled for the week of January 15–22 at the Tradewinds Resort in St. Thomas, VI. However, we cannot process it without the expiration date of your credit card. Will you please write, fax, or call us with that information as soon as possible?

Thank you for attending to this matter. We look forward to seeing you in St. Thomas.

Sincerely,

Signature

Name
Title

31e. ORDER—PLACING (GENERIC)

Date

Name/Title
Business/Organization Name
Address
City, State ZIP

Dear *(name):*

We would like to order the *(name and identification number of objects)* as listed in your *(source of listing).* The *(source)* lists *(name of objects)* as *(price per object and total price of order).* The *(source)* also indicates *(amount)* per *(object)* in shipping charges, for a total cost of *(total of order price and shipping charges).*

Please ship the *(object)* to:

> *Shipping address, including*
> *Name/Title*
> *Department*
> *Facility Name*
> *Street Address*
> *City, State ZIP*

Please send the invoice to:

> *Invoicing address, including*
> *Name/Title*
> *Department*
> *Facility Name*
> *Street Address*
> *City, State ZIP*

Please attend to this order immediately and ship via *(indicate special shipping instructions).*

Sincerely,

Signature

Name
Title

32a. PAYMENTS—ENCLOSED

Date

Name/Title
Business/Organization Name
Address
City, State ZIP

Dear *(name):*

This letter acknowledges receipt of *(object of order).* The enclosed payment
recognizes that the order was processed properly, arrived in a timely manner, and
met our specifications.

Our receiving department subjects all incoming orders to close scrutiny. The fact
that the department passed this invoice on for payment without comment indicates
an above-average level of service and satisfaction. We wanted you to know that we
are pleased with your performance as a new supplier to this firm.

We look forward to doing more business and placing additional orders with you in
the future.

Sincerely,

Signature

Name
Title

32b. PAYMENTS—DELAYING

Date

Name/Title
Business/Organization Name
Address
City, State ZIP

Dear *(name):*

We received your shipment of *(name of object)* on *(date)*. But because of what we perceive to be either a misorder or a processing error, we will be delaying payment until our staff has had a chance to examine the shipment more closely.

While the merchandise is clearly up to your usual standard of quality, it's not quite what we expected when we ordered it. Not only doesn't it match previously existing stock in size, quantity, or color, but it also doesn't match our perception of the goods we thought we had ordered.

The proper department is taking immediate steps to match the merchandise to our needs. If it is found to be acceptable, we will send a check immediately. If it is not, and if the order error is ours, we will return the merchandise at our expense. If the error is yours, we will contact you to determine the carrier by which you want it shipped and whom to tell the carrier to bill at your firm.

Thank you for your patience in this matter. We will contact you shortly with our decision.

Regards,

Signature

Name
Title

32c. PAYMENTS—REFUSING/RETURNING

Date

Name/Title
Business/Organization Name
Address
City, State ZIP

Dear *(name):*

An unanticipated shipment of *(object)* arrived at our door on *(date)*. While we have been a steady customer for this product over the past two years, our records show no indication that we had placed this order. Furthermore, the price per object for this shipment is significantly higher than the price we have been paying for similar goods over for the past year. It looks like someone has gotten his or her wires crossed.

An invoice for *(amount)* accompanied the shipment, but we have told our accounting office not to pay it. The invoice will be returned with the shipment, which currently is occupying valuable space in our warehouse.

Please contact us immediately and tell us the carrier by which you would like the shipment. We understand that such mistakes happen, but we have no intention of accepting and paying for goods we did not order.

Sincerely,

Signature

Name
Title

32d. PAYMENTS—MADE ON COMPLETION

Date

Name/Title
Business/Organization Name
Address
City, State ZIP

Dear *(name)*:

Our shipping department has indicated that it received the second of four shipments of *(name of object)* on *(date)*. This coincides with our records confirming the content and amount of the order.

On that same date, our accounting department received an invoice for the first two orders. It was part of our negotiated agreement that payment for all orders was due upon acceptance of the fourth order. We have no record of agreeing to payments midway through the delivery process. Therefore, we wait for an invoice after delivery of the last order.

If your records show something else, we will be happy to discuss the matter with you. We will look forward to the third shipment, due *(date)*, and will generate payment for the entire order with the acceptance of the fourth shipment, expected on *(date)*.

Sincerely,

Signature

Name
Title

32e. PAYMENTS—CHALLENGING

Date

Name/Title
Business/Organization Name
Address
City, State ZIP

Dear *(name):*

Your anticipated shipment of *(object)* arrived on *(date)* as expected. The quantity, quality, and selection all match those outlined in our original order. However, the price per piece was listed at *(price per piece),* for a total cost of *(total amount).* That's little a less than 30 percent higher than the price we agreed upon according to our records, which show a per-unit cost of *(amount),* for a total anticipated cost of *(total amount)* plus shipping.

We find the invoiced amount unacceptable and have instructed accounting not to process payment. Please contact us within ten days with an explanation and corrected invoice. We've enjoyed doing business with your firm, but we will be unable to continue doing so until this issue has been addressed.

Thank you for your assistance. We look forward to hearing from you.

Sincerely,

Signature

Name
Title

33a. Permission—Requesting, To Excerpt Oral Material

Date

Name/Title
Business/Organization Name
Address
City, State ZIP

Dear *(name):*

During your speech at Tuesday's Chamber of Commerce meeting, you described the plight of several area businesses that had been hit by a recent spate of burglaries, petty thefts, and vandalism. One story was especially poignant. It had to do with an elderly Latvian grocer and his wife who were the victims of repeated minor criminal abuse, and were eventually forced to close their store because of their financial inability to keep up with the losses.

This particular story exemplifies the growing prevalence of criminal activity, the threat to people of all ages and especially to the elderly, and the decay of modern society as seen through the eyes of someone who has spent many years living in it. I would like your permission to use that anecdote both in a presentation to the City Council and in some written materials I am preparing for several meetings coming up.

You may be fully credited as the source of the information, or I will be happy to keep you anonymous, depending on your wishes. Many people have a way with words, but few can touch both the intellect and the emotion as well as you have with your story. It is something I think needs to be repeated to remind all of us of what's going on out there.

Thank you in advance for your permission, and thank you for an excellent presentation. I have included two copies of this letter; please sign both and return one copy to me indicating your agreement.

Best regards,

Signature

Name
Title

Permission is given as stipulated.

_____   _____
Signature   Date

33b. Permission—Generic Requesting, to Excerpt Written Material

Date

Name/Title
Business/Organization Name
Address
City, State ZIP

Dear *(name):*

I am the author of *(name of book)* to be published by *(name of publisher)* in *(date of publication)*. The book will be approximately *(number of pages)* pages long. As part of this book, I wish to include an excerpt from your work.

I would therefore like permission to reprint *(author, title of article, magazine, date, pages or author, title of book, page numbers to excerpt, and copyright date).*

The author and publisher will receive full credit in the book. If it will be necessary to obtain permission from another source, please give me the address of that source:

_____

_____

_____

I have included a release form below for your convenience. If there is a special credit line, be sure to give me that. The copy is for your files.

Sincerely,

Signature

Name
Title

Permission is granted for use of the material as stipulated.

Date:_____   Signature:_____

Title:_____

33c. Permission—Request for More Information

Date

Name/Title
Business/Organization Name
Address
City, State ZIP

Dear *(name):*

Thank you for your recent query and interest in "From Killing to Cooperation." The author and editorial board of *Swords into Plowshares* are flattered by your request.

Because of our strict editorial policy, however, we require more information about your project before we can grant reprint permission. How much of the article do you want to reprint, or will the material be used simply as a resource? In what form will the material appear, and will you be illustrating it with the same photos or photos similar to those run in the original magazine?

We would also like to know more about your project, including the scope and context of the book, as well as a rough editorial outline and a brief list of other sources you plan to tap. As you no doubt have guessed, *Swords into Plowshares* is dedicated to the end of armed strife and the emergence of peaceful coexistence. We are unable to participate in anything that does not further those stated goals.

Thank you for your cooperation. Good luck on your project. We look forward to your response.

Pax vobiscum,

Signature

Name
Title

33d. PERMISSION—DENYING

Date

Name/Title
Business/Organization Name
Address
City, State ZIP

Dear *(name)*:

We thank you for your extensive outline and materials describing the content of your new text, *Freedom to Live, Freedom to Choose.* However, because of the militant nature of your tome, we cannot grant permission to excerpt "From Killing to Cooperation," which appeared in the December issue of *Swords into Plowshares.*

Our editorial mission is to promote peaceful coexistence and an end to armed strife. Certain portions of your book not only did not sound supportive of our goal, but gave the impression that you were trying to promote continued conflict as a form of political natural selection. That position is antithetical to all we stand for, and it would be not only inappropriate but hypocritical of us to be included in such a work.

We are sorry we could not be more cooperative. We are equally sorry that you seem to want to support a conflict that, for all intents and purposes, is drawing to a close.

Pax vobiscum,

Signature

Name
Title

34a. POLICY STATEMENTS—STANDARD

MEMORANDUM

TO:　　　　All Personnel
FROM:　　 Executive Office
DATE:
SUBJECT:　No Smoking Policy

In the interest of good health for all employees, Westcot Industries has enacted a formal No Smoking Policy for its executive offices, production facilities, and branch offices around the country. This policy takes effect at midnight May 31.

Health care specialists have proved beyond doubt that smoking is harmful to the general health of both the smoker and those working around him or her. In the interest of the well-being of all employees, no smoking will be permitted on company property before, during, or after formal work hours. This policy extends to management, staff, visitors, suppliers, and family.

In addition, Westcot Industries has enacted a policy of reimbursing employees for the costs of all recognized smoking cessation classes or workshops for themselves and their immediate families. Our purpose is not to penalize employees who smoke, but to help them develop a more healthful lifestyle.

Any questions about this or any other company policy should be referred to the executive offices.

34b. POLICY STATEMENTS—CHANGES

MEMORANDUM

TO:　　　　All Personnel
FROM:　　 Executive Office
DATE:
SUBJECT:　Changes in Employee Parking Privileges

Because of resurfacing and refurbishing of the central parking structure, there have been several changes in employee parking options. Your supervisor will brief you in greater detail, but we also wanted to explain these changes in writing in an attempt to avoid any confusion.

The central structure will be under refurbishment from June 1 to August 15. During that period, employees who normally park on floors two through four will need to park in a special section of the city lot at the corner of Adams and Mason Streets. Supervisors will issue permits so that employees will not be charged for parking. Management staff who park on the first floor may continue to do so.

We apologize for any inconvenience this change may cause. Rest assured that it will be temporary. Any questions should be referred to your supervisor or the executive offices.

34c. Policy Statements—Public Statement

Date

Name/Title
Business/Organization Name
Address
City, State ZIP

Dear *(name):*

Thank you for your inquiry about Magma Corporation's Clean Air Policy. Having once been this community's top producer of airborne pollutants, we are sensitive to our community and ecological obligations. We are also very proud of our clean-up record over the past five years.

Our policy, part of an overall corporate statement and mission, refers at length to technical standards by which Magma may operate. But the heart of the matter is that, essentially, Magma will do no materials processing, packaging, or shipping that in any way violates the minimum standards for particulate parts per thousand of untreated pollutants released into the air or water supply set by the Environmental Protection Agency. Shift managers failing to comply with these standards are subject to immediate discipline and possible dismissal.

We hope this answers your question. If we can further clarify this policy or the goals of the corporation's efforts, and its community obligations, please feel free to contact us. Thank you for your interest in Magma Corporation.

Sincerely,

Signature

Name
Title

35d. Promotions/Transfers—Rejecting

MEMORANDUM

TO: Derek Uttley, Sales Manager
FROM: Kitty Fosby, Regional Vice President
DATE:
SUBJECT: Patience Is a Virtue

Your enthusiasm—like your sales record—is to be commended, Derek. Even on what I consider to be the industry's most successful sales force, few are as forthright and purposeful as you. I wish I had another dozen like you to help Kumquat Software conquer the world.

We are currently at a crossroads in our national sales development strategy, and the department may undergo significant changes before we are through. We are currently reviewing Bob Benjamin's former position as that too may undergo significant change. If you can be patient with us during this internal process, my guess is that an energetic go-getter like you will be amply rewarded.

I will keep your proposal and your interest in mind, Derek. In the interim, keep hammering away at the Northeast. I understand that the Persimmon Group sees what it thinks is a major opportunity in several major cities. You may find the next several months both challenging and rewarding in their own way.

MEMORANDUM

TO: Derek Uttley, Sales Manager
FROM: Kitty Fosby, Regional Vice President
DATE:
SUBJECT: New Markets, New Conquests

Your enthusiasm—like your sales record—is to be commended, Derek. Even on what I consider to be the industry's most aggressive sales force, few are as forthright and purposeful as you. I wish I had another dozen like you to help Kumquat Software conquer the world.

We are currently at a crossroads in our national sales development strategy, and the department may undergo significant changes before we are through. We are reviewing Bob Benjamin's former position as that too may undergo significant change. If you can be patient with us during this internal growth process, my guess is that an energetic go-getter like you will be amply rewarded.

In the interim, we want you to consider transfering to the Southwest to help what has become a painfully sluggish market there. The economy is not as bad as it is in your previous territory, but the region presents its own challenges, including the prevalence of several Phoenix-based software providers and a particularly creative programmer in Santa Fe whom we may want to get on our side. By accepting this transfer, you will be helping Kumquat tremendously. This will also give you a taste of another region so that, when new paths are decided upon, you will have a broader range of experience.

Please set up an appointment with my assistant, Shelly Shoemaker, so that we can talk about this further. I see good things on the horizon for you, Derek, if you can wait just a little longer.

36a. PUBLIC RELATIONS—NEWS RELEASE

Note: News releases should carefully include who, what, when, where, how, and why to be most useful to the news media.

Date

For Immediate Release For further information, contact:
Media Relations Director
(212) 555-1234

QUANTAFIRM ANNOUNCES DIVIDEND

SALT LAKE CITY, UT—QuantaFirm, the nation's leading supplier of electrical components for high-tech and aerospace products, has announced a $1.45 dividend on each share of common stock. The dividend will be payable at the end of July to all stockholders of record on June 30, 19__.

The dividend comes at the end of an especially profitable fiscal year. Growing demand worldwide for QuantaFirm components has rocketed the 200-employee manufacturer from 16th to 9th place in an industry known for rapid-fire growth. The company's strategic plan calls for continued growth, despite the uneven economy.

# # #

36b. PUBLIC RELATIONS—MEDIA ALERT

Date

For further information, contact:
Media Relations Director
(212) 555-1234

QUANTAFIRM'S NEW PRODUCT MONITORS CANCER VICTIMS

WHO: QuantaFirm, a major manufacturer of electrical components.

WHAT: Unveiling of a new product to monitor cancer sufferers' vital signs and increase the likelihood of successful prognosis and treatment.

WHEN: August 1, 1995, 2:00 p.m.

WHERE: QuantaFirm International Headquarters
1226 Bullock Ave., Salt Lake City, UT.

HOW: Media conference and audiovisual presentation.

 FOR MORE INFORMATION: Contact the Media Relations Director
(212) 555-1234

# # #

36c. Public Relations—Corporate Profile for Publicity Use

The QuantaFirm Corporation was founded as a small family electronics company in Medford, Ore., by Jonathan Staley in 1982. Its purpose from the start was to explore new options for emerging electronic technologies, especially related to high-tech and aerospace alternatives. In 1986, Staley moved his firm to the more urban Salt Lake City area in hopes of capitalizing on the region's burgeoning computer peripherals industry. In 1989, the firm went public, with shares traded on the New York Stock Exchange.

Staley remains the majority stockholder and still serves as chairman, president, and chief executive officer. As electronics technology has evolved, his interest has turned from the declining aerospace industry to the realm of high-tech health care, particularly the area of cancer diagnosis and treatment. In 1992, a prototype of CancerScan, the firm's new high-tech cancer treatment and screening technology was developed. The first version for public usage was ready in March of 1994.

QuantaFirm now counts among its areas of expertise health care, aerospace, consumer electronics, and personal computers.

37a. PUBLISHING—QUERY FOR GUIDELINES/SAMPLE ISSUE

Date

Name/Title
Business/Organization Name
Address
City, State ZIP

Dear *(name)*:

As a long-time reader of *Coffee Growers Journal,* I have come to rely on the publication as the single most important resource for coffee growers, roasters, and shippers in the world. I also have spent twenty-two years in the coffee trade and have several ideas that I think would make excellent feature stories.

Please send me a set of writers' guidelines outlining requirements for submission. I also would appreciate three back issues, for which I have enclosed $4 each. You should find a check for $12 with this letter.

Your magazine has made major contributions to communications within the coffee industry. I think my article ideas will help you continue your mission and better serve fellow coffee growers.

Thank you for your prompt attention to this matter.

Sincerely,

Signature

Name
Title

37b. Publishing—Response to Query for Guidelines/Sample Issue

Date

Name/Title
Business/Organization Name
Address
City, State ZIP

Dear *(name):*

Thank you for your interest in submissions to *Coffee Growers Journal.* As requested, you will find writers' guidelines enclosed. Your request for back issues was forwarded to our circulation department for processing. Please contact us if you have not received your issues in two to four weeks.

The guidelines outline what we require of our submissions, but there is one point we need to stress. When querying us, please put all ideas in writing. Include a detailed outline if possible and the names and telephone numbers of sources you plan to interview. Too many writers, especially new contributors, try to sell us story ideas over the telephone. It is too hard for us to evaluate the concept without seeing something in writing. It also indicates how much thought you have given the idea. The more complete your outline is, the more likely it is that we will use the story.

This does not extend to completed manuscripts, however, and we would caution you not to do a story on speculation. There is a good chance that we have covered the concept, or that we already have someone working on a similar story. A query with a detailed outline will let us decide if we are interested without causing you a lot of unnecessary work. Furthermore, we may see another story concept in the outline, making the final assignment into something completely different.

Please refer to the writers' guidelines for other limitations and opportunities. We look forward to hearing your thoughts and, we hope, seeing your byline in *Coffee Growers Journal.*

Sincerely,

Signature

Name
Title

37C. PUBLISHING—QUERY FOR ARTICLE

Date

Name/Title
Business/Organization Name
Address
City, State ZIP

Dear *(name):*

Thank you for sending writers' guidelines for *Coffee Growers Journal.* I have reviewed them carefully and have come up with an idea in which I think you may be interested.

We all know how deviations in weather affect coffee prices worldwide. When the harvest is good, prices remain reasonable and stable; when drought or excessive rain affects the growth cycle of the beans, the harvest is less and prices rise accordingly. The industry even has measured the effects that interruptions in agriculture resulting from war and social unrest have on a country's coffee exports.

Little has been written, however, on the effects that rain forest depletion will have on coffee-growing practice and prices. Environmentalists have made the world aware of a tragedy in the making, but few experts have discussed the effects on individual agricultural crops. Bananas, cocoa, and coffee are three products whose environment, price, and exportability will be affected by loss of the rain forest.

I already have interviewed several environmentalists in Central and South America and have gotten some dire predictions, including:

● The effects of loss of the climatic stabilization necessary for significant coffee harvests.

● The effects of soil erosion and runoff into rivers and streams that are used to irrigate coffee plantations.

● And, finally, the net effect a changing economy will have on coffee-growing nations.

In addition to environmentalists, I also have in mind interviewing three separate coffee growers and brokers, as well as a social scientist from Lima who predicts that disruption in the coffee market will displace tens of thousands of workers and affect local economies by millions of dollars. A complete list of prospective sources and telephone numbers is enclosed.

This is an article about a trend of vital world importance that coffee growers may not yet have considered in terms of their own well-being, and it is a story that needs to be told. I think it will affect the way this important segment of our population looks at its business and the world we live in.

Please let me know what you think of the idea. I look forward to making contributions to *Coffee Growers Journal,* and I would like this to be the first.

Thank you for your consideration.

Best regards,

Signature

Name
Title

37d. PUBLISHING—RESPONSE TO ARTICLE QUERY (POSITIVE)

Date

Name/Title
Business/Organization Name
Address
City, State ZIP

Dear *(name):*

Thank you for your query about how rain forest depletion will affect the coffee industry. We find the idea appealing and of significant importance, and we would like to urge you to go ahead with it for publication in *Coffee Growers Journal.*

There is no doubt a great deal you can write on the subject, but we encourage you to keep your piece to about 2,500 words in length. We require all articles to be submitted both as hard copy and on computer disk. We have translation software that can deal with almost any commercial word processing program.

As a scholarly journal, we pay an honorarium of only $250 for an article of this length, but we can supply you with up to twenty copies of the article for your personal use. We hope this is satisfactory.

We have scheduled your story for the November/December issue, which means we will need it no later than September 15. If this deadline cannot be met, let us know and we will reschedule your piece. Please also let us know about any sources of photos of which you may be aware. We will handle the actual acquisition, but your assistance would be helpful. If you have taken any photos yourself that you would like considered, please feel free to enclose them with your manuscript.

Thanks again for your interest. We look forward to your submission.

Best regards,

Signature

Name
Title

37e. PUBLISHING—RESPONSE TO ARTICLE QUERY [NEGATIVE]

Date

Name/Title
Business/Organization Name
Address
City, State ZIP

Dear *(name):*

Thank you for your query about how rain forest depletion will affect the coffee industry. Unfortunately, this is something we have covered in varying ways and to varying degrees over the past two years. Recently Costa Rica, Honduras, and Peru all have enacted legislation designed to protect cash crops like coffee, cocoa, bananas, and betel nut. We have reported on this legislation and its effects in the past two issues.

We appreciate the thought and research, especially the work you have done with the Lima social scientist. One facet of coffee production we have given little attention has been the effect of industry changes on workers and, conversely, the effect that changes in the workforce have had on the coffee industry. Up to now we have lacked an authoritative source, but it sounds like this social scientist may be the type of person we have been seeking.

Would you be interested in researching this idea a little further and talking to your Lima contact? If this person turns up the type of information to which we think he or she may have access, then we may just have an article assignment for you.

Thanks again for your interest. We look forward to hearing from you soon.

Regards,

Signature

Name
Title

38a. PURCHASES—REQUEST (ADVERTISED DISCOUNT)

Date

Name/Title
Business/Organization Name
Address
City, State ZIP

Dear *(name):*

The recent issue of *(name of publication)* advertised your *(name and description of product)* at a discount price of *(cost or percentage of discount)*. If it is not too late, we would like to order *(number)* of this product.

As prices continue to to climb, such special discounts not only help us better manage valuable resources, but show support on your part of the growing challenges facing businesses and consumers alike. We appreciate such money-saving opportunities, and will be more inclined to do business with *(name of company)* in the future.

We look forward to the shipment of *(name of product)*. Please notify us directly of similar specials on this or any of your line of *(generic description of merchandise)*.

Thank you for your assistance.

Sincerely,

Signature

Name
Title

38b. Purchases—Request (Unadvertised Discount)

Date

Name/Title
Business/Organization Name
Address
City, State ZIP

Dear *(name)*:

Competition within the *(name of industry)* industry has led to price wars of significant magnitude in the last *(time period)*. Although you have advertised many of your products at a discount, your *(name of product)* remains listed at full retail price. Unfortunately, that's a price we feel may soon put it out of the range of most customers.

We prefer using *(name of product)*, but we also are feeling the financial crunch affecting most of the *(name of industry)* industry. Sale prices on your other products reflect a corporate flexibility designed to help your customers cope with financial stress. We wondered if the price for *(name of product)*, if bought in sufficient quantity, was equally flexible. Right now we have a need for twelve gross of *(name of product)*, and we would like to know the best price you can give us on the purchase.

We prefer doing business with *(name of company)* and, at the right price for *(name of product)*, will continue to do so. Our purchasing department has located several substitute products at significantly lower cost that, while not preferable, will perform the function satisfactorily. If your price remains inflexible, we may be forced to make a switch.

We hope you understand the dilemma we face. And we look forward to a prompt response to our inquiry. Thank you.

Regards,

Signature

Name
Title

38C. PURCHASES—RESPONSE (FAVORABLE)

Date

Name/Title
Business/Organization Name
Address
City, State ZIP

Dear *(name)*:

Your recent letter of *(date)* put our executive team in a bit of a squeeze. How best can we continue serving good customers when we ourselves are caught in a financial bind? After a review of your purchase records and a reexamination of our good past relationship, we have decided that loyalty and service mean more than short-term profits.

Regarding *(name of product)*, we would be delighted to make your firm a special offer of *(price)* per unit, a discount of *(percent)* below the advertised price. In order to help us keep our books in order, we ask that you purchase eighteen gross rather than twelve gross. The additional quantity will help offset the loss of income we will realize from this discount.

If these terms are satisfactory, do nothing more. The eighteen gross will be shipped on *(date)*. If there are special shipping instructions, please call *(name)* at *(telephone number)* immediately. *(He/she)* will be happy to assist in making the necessary arrangements you will need.

Payment, as always, will be net due in thirty days. Thank you for inquiry and your willingness to work with us through hard times.

Sincerely,

Signature

Name
Title

38d. PURCHASES—RESPONSE (UNFAVORABLE)

Date

Name/Title
Business/Organization Name
Address
City, State ZIP

Dear *(name):*

Thank you for your interest in *(name of product)*. As a discount supplier of *(nature of merchandise)*, we base our prices on arrangements we make with individual manufacturers. Therefore, we are unable to reduce the cost of *(name of product)* below the already discounted list price of *(amount)*. We apologize of if is inconvenient, but unfortunately it is the best we can do.

In general, such a policy serves us and our customers well by allowing us to offer the lowest available list price on all merchandise. Occasionally, however, it backfires on us by taking away the flexibility we need to respond to customers like you. We are sorry we cannot offer more in this case.

We value your business and look forward to serving you again. In the meantime, we hope you understand the predicament we face.

Sincerely,

Signature

Name
Title

38e. Purchases—Shipment Not Arrived

Date

Name/Title
Business/Organization Name
Address
City, State ZIP

Dear *(name)*:

On *(date)*, we ordered *(quantity)* of *(name of products)* as listed in *(place of listing or advertisement)* and priced at *(cost)*. To date, the shipment has not yet arrived.

We understand that handling and processing take time, but we think *(length of delay)* is far too long and fear that something has happened to our shipment. Please check your records to see if the order has been processed and shipped. If not, please take care of this without further delay.

Thank you for your immediate attention to this matter.

Sincerely,

Signature

Name
Title

38f. Purchases—Shipping Delay [More Information]

Date

Name/Title
Business/Organization Name
Address
City, State ZIP

Dear *(name)*:

With regard to your letter of *(date)* we have no record of your order of *(date)* for *(name and quantity of product)*. If anything was lost in the mail, it must have been your original order.

Please send us a copy of your original purchase order or a new one for *(name of product)* and we will be happy to process it immediately.

We regret any inconveniences caused by this delay and look forward to serving you.

Sincerely,

Signature

Name
Title

38g. PURCHASES—HAS BEEN SHIPPED

Date

Name/Title
Business/Organization Name
Address
City, State ZIP

Dear *(name)*:

Thank you for your letter of *(date)* regarding your order for *(name and quantity of product)*. Our internal research has uncovered a bottleneck in our fulfillment procedures that has delayed several shipments, including yours. The error has been rectified and will not occur again. Your order has now been processed and shipped.

Please accept our apologies for the delay. If any more problems occur with either this or other orders, please contact me, and I will personally take care of the matter.

Sincerely,

Signature

Name
Title

38h. PURCHASES—HAS BEEN BACK-ORDERED

Date

Name/Title
Business/Organization Name
Address
City, State ZIP

Dear *(name)*:

Thank you for your letter of *(date)* regarding your order for *(name and quantity of product)*. This product has proved very popular, and we have been unable to keep a sufficient supply in stock. We will fill your order as soon as stock arrives.

We apologize for any inconvenience and appreciate your patience and patronage.

Sincerely,

Signature

Name
Title

—REQUESTING [CANDIDATE]

Name/Title
Business/Organization Name
Address
City, State ZIP

Dear *(name):*

It has been my good fortune to have known you in both a personal and a professional capacity for many years. I have always respected your judgment and your leadership, and hoped that some day I would have the chance to take on responsibilities similar to yours and, with any luck, do them half as well. That day appears to have come.

A large firm has heard of my experience working under your guidance, and I have been asked to interview for the position of controller. I would like to give your name as a reference.

I expect no preferential treatment and just ask you to relay your experience with me and my performance when I worked for you. You are well respected in the industry and someone whom many of us trust implicitly. I know you will give an accurate picture of my abilities.

My first interview is next week, with follow-up shortly thereafter if all goes well. If it turns out that we are serious about each other, I would expect them to contact you within two weeks.

Thanks for the consideration and, again, for your help and inspiration over the years.

Best regards,

Signature

Name

39b. References—Requesting (Employer)

Date

Name/Title
Business/Organization Name
Address
City, State ZIP

Dear *(name):*

John Allen Smith has applied for the position of controller with this firm and has listed you as one of his primary references. According to Mr. Smith, he worked with your firm first as staff accountant, then as chief accountant from 1988 to 1994.

Would you be so kind as to complete the attached form outlining Mr. Smith's responsibilities and quality of work for your firm? We are especially interested in his ability to manage staff, handle stress, and interact with other departments. We appreciate any information you may be willing to share.

Thank you for your assistance.

Sincerely,

Signature

Name
Title

39c. References—Responding (Candidate)

Date

Name/Title
Business/Organization Name
Address
City, State ZIP

Dear *(name):*

I am happy to serve as a reference for you. I always appreciated your hard work on our behalf and felt you made solid contributions when you were employed here. I am glad I now have the chance to help you.

If I were to be asked, I would describe you as committed, a very hard and smart worker, and a team player on whom all of us could reliably count. You are a master of your profession, and you have an intuitive understanding of both numbers and people that have made you especially effective in staff and project management situations. You are also personable, reliable, and a pleasure to work with.

How is that for a start?

Sincerely,

Signature

Name
Title

39d. REFERENCES—RESPONDING FAVORABLY (EMPLOYER)

Date

Name/Title
Business/Organization Name
Address
City, State ZIP

Dear *(name):*

John Allen Smith did indeed work for this firm during the years and in the capacity you say in your recent letter. And I am pleased to recommend him for your controller position.

During his seven years with our firm, Mr. Smith showed much skill in managing both the numbers and the people who produce them. He has an innate ability to get to the heart of matters, and knows how to work with people, rather than against them, to achieve his goals. He was well respected by his colleagues and our clients, and we were sorry to see him leave.

He has managed numerous projects, some under extreme stress, and always has performed in an exemplary fashion. His management skills show an unusual maturity, and his coworkers speak highly of his ability to stimulate effort and promote enthusiasm in the projects he has managed.

If you need further information, please do not hesitate to contact me directly. I will be happy to speak to you at length about Mr. Smith's qualifications.

Sincerely,

Signature

Name
Title

39e. REFERENCES—RESPONDING NEUTRALLY (EMPLOYER)

Date

Name/Title
Business/Organization Name
Address
City, State ZIP

Dear *(name):*

John Allen Smith worked for this firm in the position first of staff accountant and later of chief accountant during the period 1988 to 1994. During that period he was promoted three times, with appropriate salary increases accompanying each level of promotion.

Earlier this year, Mr. Smith left our employment to begin his own business.

Sincerely,

Signature

Name
Title

39f. REFERENCES—DECLINING (EMPLOYER)

Date

Name/Title
Business/Organization Name
Address
City, State ZIP

Dear *(name):*

We received your letter requesting further information and a recommendation for John Allen Smith. We respectfully decline to fulfill your request.

It is company policy that we supply no references, either good or bad, for past employees. Our attorneys inform us that such references can be the basis for legal action by both candidates and hiring firms who believe that the information presented in the recommendation was inaccurate. We have no wish to have that happen in this or any other case.

Please realize that this is company policy and no reflection on either Mr. Smith or his performance. We are sorry we could not be of more assistance.

Sincerely,

Signature

Name
Title

39g. References—Thank You for the Reference

Date

Name/Title
Business/Organization Name
Address
City, State ZIP

Dear *(name):*

As my first act as controller for this firm, I want to personally write and thank you for what must have been an exceptionally strong endorsement and recommendation. According to my new employer, your recommendation swayed the final decision. I am greatly indebted to you for that.

When I first applied for this job, a friend asked who I was using as references, and I told him I would only use those people for whom I have the greatest respect. I am glad I stuck to my guns on that one, because it appears that the respect is mutual.

Thanks again for your help. I sincerely appreciate your support.

With best regards,

Signature

Name
Title

40a. REFERRALS—REQUESTING

Date

Name/Title
Business/Organization Name
Address
City, State ZIP

Dear *(name)*:

As the Xylon Corporation's chief legal counsel, I have enjoyed working with you and the rest of the staff for the last eight years. Establishing my own law practice was something about which I only dreamed. It was your encouragement and support that made the transition possible. I cannot thank you enough for that.

As a new solo practitioner, I am looking for more opportunities to serve the same industry. I hope I will be able to assist Xylon's staff lawyers from time to time in any legal matters for which my background and experience is appropriate. I also hope you will think to refer me to any of your client or supplier firms in need of legal assistance or services.

I already have several clients interested in retaining my firm based on the work I did for Xylon. May I use you and fellow executive staff members with whom I have worked closely as personal references to these new clients? Your continued support is greatly appreciated.

Sincerely,

Signature

Name
Title

40b. REFERRALS—OFFERING

Date

Name/Title
Business/Organization Name
Address
City, State ZIP

Dear *(name):*

There is nothing quite like starting your own business to get your heart pumping and your blood flowing, and to help you find repeated opportunities to sit bolt upright in bed seized in the grip of fear.

Seriously, we all wish you the very best of success. Self-employment takes no small amount of courage, but those who are good at what they do are nearly always rewarded. We have every reason to believe that your star will climb even higher as you become more involved with running your own business.

If this company or any of its executives can do anything to help generate or promote business for you, feel free to call on us. We are happy to provide references, referrals, and anything else you may need to make this new venture a success.

Best of luck. We know we will be hearing from you.

Best regards,

Signature

Name
Title

41a. REMINDERS—OF MEETINGS

MEMORANDUM

TO: Senior Staff
FROM: *(Name)*
DATE:
SUBJECT: Planning Meeting

This is to remind you of the budget and strategic planning meeting scheduled for Thursday, September 16, at 9 a.m. The meeting will start promptly at that time and continue until noon or until all items on the attached agenda have been addressed.

Come prepared to discuss proposed staff travel, major purchase plans, and revenue lines on the preliminary budgets you have already submitted. Next year looks to be tight, so be prepared to defend all requests beyond nominal 4 percent increases.

My secretary has reserved the conference room on the third floor for our meeting.

41b. REMINDERS—OF AN OBLIGATION

MEMORANDUM

TO: Vice President/Human Resources
FROM: *(Name)*
DATE:
SUBJECT: Upcoming Sensitivity Training Session

This is a reminder of your scheduled participation in the sexual harassment staff sensitivity session scheduled for next Wednesday in the Flagler Auditorium. You will be joining Chief Counsel Melanie Harris and President Boris Russo for a roundtable discussion from 2 to 3 p.m.

Your role will be to discuss alternatives available through the HR office for dealing with sexual harassment and disciplinary actions to be taken against offenders. This is an important issue, and we appreciate your time and participation in this vital training event.

41c. REMINDERS—OF AN APPOINTMENT

MEMORANDUM

TO: President's Office
FROM: *(Name)*
DATE:
SUBJECT: Gearbox Industries Meeting Reminder

Before we get too caught up in planning sessions for next year, I need to remind President Obie that he has an appointment to meet with representatives from Gearbox Industries about our participation in their upcoming retooling plans. The meeting will take place Monday afternoon at 2 p.m. at Gearbox headquarters, 4321 Isotope Lane. I have prepared an overview of the firm as well as some comparative analyses of how we might help Gearbox with its plans. I will be available to discuss these things at President Obie's convenience.

41d. REMINDERS—OF A DOCUMENT/PROCEDURE

MEMORANDUM

TO: All Staff
FROM: *(Name)*
DATE:
SUBJECT: No Smoking Policy Reminder

Just a reminder that, beginning Monday, this company will enact a formal no smoking policy for its executive, manufacturing, and shipping facilities. No smoking will be allowed anywhere on company premises, and encouragement and financial assistance will be available to those who wish to quit smoking through a recognized clinical or therapeutic program. We are not attempting to penalize those employees that do smoke. We only want to encourage the best possible health among all our workers.

41e. REMINDERS—OF A DEADLINE

MEMORANDUM

TO: Executive Staff
FROM: *(Name)*
DATE:
SUBJECT: Budget Deadlines

This is to remind you that all preliminary budgets are due no later than September 18. Chief Financial Officer Ed Stilt will create spreadsheets for each department integrating other departments' needs. You then will be able to work on your budget and see how your actions affect others. Final budgets will be due October 31.

42a. Reprimands—Gentle

MEMORANDUM

TO: Operations Manager
FROM: *(Name)*
DATE:

Lately it has come to our attention that the reports you have been giving at managerial meetings have not been up to your usual standard. Several other managers attempted to follow through on certain project steps based on your analyses and found that information was either missing or inaccurate. In one case, a report of yours stated that the project already had been taken through steps your staff had not yet even attempted. The net result was not only wasted time and effort but the concern that serious deficiencies could have developed had some of your instructions been followed.

This surprises me because it is so unlike you. Your past work shows exceptional quality and very thorough attention to detail. I might have suspected this lapse from several employees at this firm, but you would not have been one of them.

We all go through personal and professional crises in our lives occasionally, and perhaps one such crisis is affecting your performance. If you would like to discuss it, you know my door is open. If you need to take time off to handle any problems, feel free to do that, too. Yours is a very important position that requires a professional at the top of his or her form. That's why we have put you in the position, and that's why we need your best performance at all times.

Let us know what we can do to help.

42b. Reprimands—Progressive Discipline, Step 1

MEMORANDUM

TO: Operations Manager
FROM: *(Name)*
DATE:

Several weeks ago we shared with you our concern over inconsistencies in your performance. We offered several alternatives and talked at length about possible solutions. Unfortunately, you elected to follow through on none of our joint suggestions, and your performance continues to suffer.

In addition to errors and inaccuracies in your work, we note that your attendance and attitude also have begun to suffer. This is not in keeping with the solutions we explored. What's more, it has begun seriously affecting the performance of your staff and the attitude of your management peers. We are unaware of the exact nature of your problem, other than that it is "personal," but we are aware of the effect it is having on others. This has to change immediately.

The company provides several viable alternatives for employees suffering from such problems, and we direct you to seek counseling anonymously with one of these firms. We further recommend that you take some of your accrued vacation time and sort these problems out. Failures in your performance can no longer be tolerated, and if you will not act on your own behalf, we will be forced to seek harsher alternatives.

42c. REPRIMANDS—PROGRESSIVE DISCIPLINE, STEP 2

MEMORANDUM

TO: Operations Manager
FROM: (Name)
DATE:

Six weeks ago we directed you to seek counseling and take some time off to address the personal problems that have been seriously affecting your performance and the morale of other employees. Despite repeated warnings, you have failed to follow those directions or take steps to improve your situation.

We have no choice but to suspend you without pay for a period of two weeks, during which time we insist that you address the issue. We also insist that you seek professional counseling; in fact, reinstatement will be dependent on your willingness to do so.

We regret that the situation has come to this, but your failure to act on your own behalf has left us no choice.

42d. REPRIMANDS—PROGRESSIVE DISCIPLINE, STEP 3: DISMISSAL

MEMORANDUM

TO: Operations Manager
FROM: (Name)
DATE:

This is to notify you formally and finally that you have been terminated as operations manager for this firm effective immediately. Continued personal problems and your failure to address them have seriously affected your ability to perform this role. What's more, misinformation in reports written by you has led to several uncomfortable and dangerous situations.

Please clean out your desk and vacate the premises as of 4:00 p.m. today.

43a. RESIGNATION—POSITIVE

MEMORANDUM

TO: President
FROM: *(Name)*
DATE:

After ten years of learning much and working hard to further the goals of this organization, I find that I am now ready to move down another path. It is with a mixture of both happiness and regret that I tender my resignation to this organization.

Certain periods of our lives are rich with experiences and opportunities. That is how the last ten years here have been. All that I have gained and have been allowed to put into practice has been noticed by a major corporation, which has offered me significant new opportunities to grow and prosper. It is something I simply cannot afford to pass up.

I offer my heartfelt thanks to those in the company who have encouraged my professional development and provided support for my initiatives over the years. I have gained a great deal from working here, and I hope I have been able to return a least part of what I have gained in loyalty and value to the firm.

43b. RESIGNATION—NEUTRAL/NEGATIVE

MEMORANDUM

TO: President
FROM: *(Name)*
DATE:

Effective June 5, I will be resigning from this company to take a position as vice president with XYZ Corporation. I appreciate the opportunities and courtesies that have been shown me during my stay here.

43c. Resignation—Acceptance (Positive)

MEMORANDUM

TO: Vice President
FROM: *(Name)*
DATE:

It is with no little pride and a sense of deep regret that we accept your resignation. You have been an influential member of our firm, and we wish you the very best in your new endeavor.

We all take many roads during our travels through life, and the luckier of us meet up with people with true quality, initiative, drive, and accomplishment. You characterize all of these things, and I am glad our paths brought us together for as long as they have. You have been a true asset to our organization, and I appreciate having been able to rely on you both personally and professionally over the years.

Please stay in touch and let us know how things are going. If there is anything we can do to ease the transition or encourage your continued growth, just call. You will always have a cheering section in this organization.

43d. Resignation—Accepting (Neutral/Negative)

MEMORANDUM

TO: Vice President
FROM: *(Name)*
DATE:

This memorandum serves as official notification of our acceptance of your resignation. Best of luck in your future endeavors.

44a. RESUME TRANSMITTAL—FOR SELF

Date

Name/Title
Business/Organization Name
Address
City, State ZIP

Dear *(name)*:

Our recent luncheon at the CEO Roundtable brought to light several mutual interests and commonalties between the work of your firm and my background and skills. I appreciated the opportunity to get to know you and learn more about your company.

Your comments about growth opportunities especially interested me. I know you are seeking to fill several new management positions, and I would like to express to you my interest in discussing the possibility of heading one of your teams. I think I have the type of experience that would benefit your efforts, including:

- 15 years staff management, with special emphasis on manufacturing, sales, and shipping.

- 8 years senior management experience in these same areas.

- 6 opportunities to head up specific task forces and work groups successfully devoted to problem solving. One of these groups was cited by former President George Bush for its contributions to our industry.

I have taken the liberty of enclosing my resume for your complete information. If you like what you see, I hope you will have your secretary call me to set up an appointment. I would relish the opportunity to explain to you how I think I could help your firm in its new initiatives.

I hope to speak with you again soon.

Best regards,

Signature

Name
Title

44b. RESUME TRANSMITTAL—FOR ANOTHER

Date

Name/Title
Business/Organization Name
Address
City, State ZIP

Dear *(name)*:

I try never to take advantage of our friendship, *(name)*, but this is one time I am going to break that rule. In fact, I am going to force a young man on you who I think is the answer to your staff management problems.

(Name of candidate) worked for me for 11 years in the area of human resources, then moved to one of our competitors. (I will not mention any names, but I think you know of whom I speak.) *(First name of candidate)* at last has come to his senses and is looking to rejoin the white hats, and I think it is a move that could greatly benefit both of you.

(First name of candidate) has the background you need to put a cap on staff attrition at your plant and get to the root of employee dissatisfaction. He has the management wherewithal and experience to take hold of the problem and successfully resolve it. Given what I know of your situation, I do not think you could ask for a better person.

Enclosed is *(candidates')* resume. I have suggested that he call within the week to set up an appointment with you so you can put these issues to rest. I suggest you not pass this young man by, *(name of addressee)*. If I had the right opening, I would have hired him back in a heartbeat.

Sincerely,

Signature

Name
Title

45a. Sales and Marketing—Telephone Call Lead-in

Date

Name/Title
Business/Organization Name
Address
City, State ZIP

Dear *(name):*

Just a note to say how much Rod and I enjoyed having dinner with you at the Advertising Club meeting last Tuesday. We always enjoy the chance to talk with you.

We enjoyed the rundown on what is happening at Laemmle Productions. Afterward we got to talking and realized that there are several new adaptations of our software product that may be just the thing to help you solve some of the problems you referred to during dinner. We would like very much to demonstrate those options to you in hopes that there may be a way we could work together in the future.

Rod will be out of town for the next two weeks, but neither he nor I felt we should wait to show you our ideas. I would like to take the liberty of calling you next week to see if we might set up an appointment and explore further options together.

Thanks for the consideration. We will be talking soon.

Best regards,

Signature

Name
Title

45b. SALES AND MARKETING—SETTING APPOINTMENT

Date

Name/Title
Business/Organization Name
Address
City, State ZIP

Dear *(name):*

The future of small engines rests not on the mechanisms that run them, but on the fuel options allowed by future federal government standards. Without the right components, your niche in the small engine market may quickly evaporate. But JetPac offers you a way to protect that niche.

JetPac representatives will be in your area participating in the National Energy Exposition next month, and we would like to show you what we can do to help your products meet the energy needs of the twenty-first century. If you can free up an hour on March 19, we can show you where our industry is going. And we may even have a way to help you get there.

Sales secretary Eileen Schmidt will call on behalf of senior associate Bob Brand on Monday, February 15. We hope you will be able to find the time to meet with Bob on March 19. It may just be the most valuable hour you will invest in your business's future this year.

Sincerely,

Signature

Name
Title

45c. Sales and Marketing—New Product

Date

Name/Title
Business/Organization Name
Address
City, State ZIP

Dear *(name):*

JetPac is here, and it may be just what you are looking for to help revolutionize
your company's small engine construction and fuel distribution in the years to
come.

Federal standards will make emission control compliance tougher for all forms of
internal combustion engines. But in 1996, the Environmental Protection Agency
will shift its sights from Detroit's automotive empire to small engine manufacturers
throughout the country. Regulators plan to take the same tough standards they have
set for automobiles and apply them to companies without the profit margins to
support major retooling efforts. Of necessity, some of these companies will go out
of business. Yours does not have to be one of those.

JetPac offers a patented fuel filtering and distribution system that removes 94
percent of all harmful and noxious gases from all sizes of internal combustion
engines. Rather than requiring complete redesign and overhaul of the
manufacturing process, JetPac's assembly procedures mesh with preexisting
assembly line operations. The JetPac filter and manifold assembly fits easily over
existing carburetors. An extra step, rather than a complete overhaul, is all that is
required.

We have enclosed detailed literature describing the product's engineering specifications, and we urge you to study it closely. If you think your production line may
have room for a JetPac assembler and you agree that your company will not survive
without some form of greater emission controls, then call our toll-free number
today and learn more about what JetPac can do to help position your product for the
twenty-first century.

Sincerely,

Signature

Name
Title

45d. SALES AND MARKETING—NEW SALES REP INTRODUCTION

Date

Name/Title
Business/Organization Name
Address
City, State ZIP

Dear *(name):*

We were excited to hear that you are interested in a demonstration of how JetPac
will enhance your internal combustion product and help you build market share.
But unlike in years past, I will not be the one making the demonstration. And I
think you will be glad that this is the case.

Sheila Marcus is one of our newest sales associates, and also one of our brightest, in
my estimation. A graduate of Northwestern University, Sheila majored in sales and
marketing. More important, however, is the time she spent with the JetPac
development team both in the lab and on the testing ground. Sheila's well versed in
what JetPac can do and can answer all your questions—technical and otherwise.

Sheila tells me she will be able to keep our 8:30 a.m. appointment next Thursday
with no trouble, and I think you will be pleased by the presentation she gives. I'm
confident you will find JetPac worth adding to your products.

Best regards,

Signature

Name
Title

45e. SALES AND MARKETING—TERRITORY REDISTRIBUTION

Date

Name/Title
Business/Organization Name
Address
City, State ZIP

Dear *(name):*

This letter announces a redistribution of sales territories for all associates working on the JetPac account. We have reviewed everyone's recent sales records and have adjusted plans in an attempt to better cover the market. In no way should this redistribution be construed as indicating dissatisfaction with your performance. We have confidence in your abilities; otherwise you would not have received this letter.

Changes effective November 1 are as follows:

- Sheila Marcus will move from our northeast to our southeast sector in an attempt to revitalize sagging sales in the market. Don Gelding, former sales manager of the southeast section, is no longer with the firm.

- Bob Brand has been promoted to national sales manager and will supervise all regional sales managers. Bob's former position as midcentral sales manager will be handled by Mary Bradley.

- Northwest manager Dennis Punzo and southwest manager Astrid Kirche will switch positions, a measure designed to increase sales dynamics within the two regions.

All positions will continue reporting directly or indirectly to the chief operating officer, Beatrice Potter. Questions may be directed either to your immediate supervisor or to me.

Sincerely,

Signature

Name
Title

Date

Name/Title
Business/Organization Name
Address
City, State ZIP

Dear *(name)*:

Thank you for letting us review Xypro Industries' inventory management system needs. We are impressed with your current operation and feel we have just the system to meet your needs.

The Wacker 4000 provides ample avenues for system management data, plus handling bays and digital storage capabilities designed to keep recordkeeping to a minimum. In addition to managing data through CD-ROM, the Wacker 4000 provides the type of material handling that offers employees a safe working environment. Our automatic telephone system also processes incoming work orders and inquiries with minimal staff involvement.

The list price on the Wacker 4000 is $34,695. But we are pleased to offer it at a demonstration price of $28,375. That includes installation and up to six training sessions for up to ten primary staff members. Additional training is available and billable at $75 per hour. On-line assistance is available at $9 per half-hour.

We believe the Wacker 4000 is the answer to your systems management needs. Please call us with your decision within ten days so we may put the technology of the future to work for you.

Best regards,

Signature

Name
Title

45g. SALES AND MARKETING—BID ACCEPTANCE

Date

Name/Title
Business/Organization Name
Address
City, State ZIP

Dear *(name):*

Our executive staff has reviewed your bid to manage Xypro Industries' system needs using the Wacker 4000. After careful examination of your engineering specifications and bid evaluation, we are pleased to report that we accept your offer.

We expect the system to be functional no later than September 1. Please coordinate the necessary timing and installation needs with Operations Manager Carl Pelky. He will provide the coordinates and schematics you will need to complete the installation and test runs.

Thank you for your interest in Xypro. We look forward to putting the Wacker 4000 through its paces.

Sincerely,

Signature

Name
Title

45h. SALES AND MARKETING—THANK YOU FOR THE SALE

Date

Name/Title
Business/Organization Name
Address
City, State ZIP

Dear *(name):*

Thank you for your recent order. Our operations managers have met with Mr. Pelky of your staff, and we are delighted to report that we will have the Wacker 4000 installed and operative by August 24, roughly a week prior to your September 1 deadline.

Now is the time to think about on-line support and training needs. If you have not selected primary operations staff for training, we recommend that you do so prior to the completion of installation. That will give us the opportunity to maximize their training on your behalf so that they are ready when you need them. We also have set up an on-line account and access for you when and if the need arises after the unit is in use.

We are delighted to be serving Xypro Industries' system management needs. Thank you again for your order. We look forward to working with you.

Best regards,

Signature

Name
Title

Date

Name/Title
Business/Organization Name
Address
City, State ZIP

Dear *(name)*:

Our engineers report that, according to Mr. Pelky of your staff, the Wacker 4000 is effectively meeting Xypro Industries' system management needs. Now that the system's probationary period is drawing to a close, we know the Wacker really will be put to the test. We look forward to seeing the results.

In the meantime, are there any other companies within your industry that you feel might benefit from a system similar to the one we installed at Xypro? We are currently looking to expand our market and see a natural fit with businesses such as yours. Any references or referrals you can share would be most appreciated.

Thanks for the assistance. Please call if we can be of additional service to Xypro Industries.

Sincerely,

Signature

Name
Title

45j. SALES AND MARKETING—GOODWILL/CORPORATE SUPPORT

Date

Name/Title
Business/Organization Name
Address
City, State ZIP

Dear *(name):*

We read with interest the article about Xypro Industries' fund drive to help feed, clothe, and house the homeless during this holiday season. You are to be commended on your humanitarian efforts.

Please accept this small donation of $250 toward your charitable work. We hope it will in some way make the lives of those who turn to you that much easier during this joyous season.

With best holiday wishes,

Signature

Name
Title

46a. SOLICITATIONS—REQUESTING

Date

Name/Title
Business/Organization Name
Address
City, State ZIP

Dear *(name)*:

As an alumnus of Balfour University, you recognize both the value of the institution and the role that institutions of higher education can play in the community. This year the gown has truly extended its hand to the town, taking up a social cause the likes of which higher education has rarely seen.

Balfour's School of Education has "adopted" Ulysses S. Grant Elementary School and turned the school into a living educational laboratory. Starting with the current first- and second-grade classes, School of Education faculty and students will tutor children, assist educators, and consult with administrators and fundraisers with an eye toward developing a 100 percent college-bound class. Those first and second graders will be monitored and assisted through seventh grade. And each first and second grade in the years to come will have its own set of educators as long as Balfour can sustain its program.

To do that, we need your help. We are seeking donations from supporters like you to help us sustain and even expand this program. We would like to suggest that you consider giving $250, but a donation of any size will be gladly accepted. Just fill in the pledge card with the proper amount.

Education is the future of this country. You can help the future of Balfour and its community by becoming involved and contributing to this program. It is for the sake of both the kids and our future.

Sincerely,

Signature

Name
Title

46b. SOLICITATIONS—QUERYING

Date

Name/Title
Business/Organization Name
Address
City, State ZIP

Dear *(name)*:

As a Balfour School of Education alumnus and current educator, I find your project intriguing and imaginative. It seems like just the thing Professor Paisley and his staff might attempt. I wish the department success.

However, I do have some concerns about the scientific methodology behind the project, as well as what seems like high donation expectations. I will gladly contribute to the program to help the kids at Grant Elementary, but not without first knowing the following:

- Who is administering the curricula—the School of Education or the teachers and administrators at Grant?

- What has been done to augment educational efforts in the pupils' homes?

- What exactly is my $250 going to go for? What is the total seed fund needed to get the project underway? Is funding coming from sources other than private donations?

If you can satisfactorily answer these questions, I will be glad to donate. Such projects can have many variables and problems. I will need to know more before I consider donating any of my hard-earned salary.

Sincerely,

Signature

Name
Title

46c. Solicitations—Responding (Positively)

Date

Name/Title
Business/Organization Name
Address
City, State ZIP

Dear *(name):*

Other than those associated with classroom survival, few educators take chances anymore. I applaud what Balfour's School of Education is attempting to do and am happy to enclose my contribution to your efforts.

Please keep me informed of your activities. If Balfour can pull off such a program in its community, there is no telling what is possible for schools across the country.

Good luck,

Signature

Name
Title

46d. Solicitations—Requesting Referrals

Date

Name/Title
Business/Organization Name
Address
City, State ZIP

Dear *(name):*

Thank you for your generous contribution to the Ulysses S. Grant Elementary School Scholarship Fund. We have already put your funds to work on the children's behalf, and the new semester in their educational laboratory already has begun.

We see a need to expand the program in order to address many of the students' home needs. We are seeking additional donations from previous contributors, or referrals to like-minded individuals who both understand and appreciate what it is that Balfour University seeks to accomplish. If you cannot contribute again so soon, would you please complete the attached card with the names and addresses of friends and relatives who you think might appreciate and support our efforts.

As in the past, we appreciate your continued support. Help us help the next generation gain better control of its own destiny.

Sincerely,

Signature

Name
Title

47a. SPEAKING ENGAGEMENTS—FAMILIAR/CASUAL

Date

Name/Title
Business/Organization Name
Address
City, State ZIP

Dear *(name):*

The head of our Kiwanis Club asked me who I thought might make a good luncheon speaker—someone who was quick on his feet, had a sense of humor, and could be counted on to inform, entertain, and, yes, even inspire with his message.

Naturally you came to mind. And we're glad you have agreed to be our speaker.

Seriously, you would be addressing a particularly astute group of businesspeople who, while they enjoy an entertaining presentation, also demand something to take home with them. I think you will do a great job, and I could not be happier that you have agreed to come.

The time is noon sharp for lunch, followed by your presentation at 12:30 p.m. The place is the Flamingo Club on Dexter Avenue. The compensation is, of course, absolutely nothing except my gratitude and appreciation.

I look forward to seeing you there, and thanks for agreeing to come.

Kindest regards,

Signature

Name
Title

47b. SPEAKING ENGAGEMENTS—UNFAMILIAR/FORMAL

Date

Name/Title
Business/Organization Name
Address
City, State ZIP

Dear *(name):*

Your expertise and reputation in urban planning precede you, and members of the National Association of City Councils know and appreciate your point of view about the plight of modern metropolitan areas. We invite you to share that point of view at the association's upcoming annual convention, scheduled for June 27–30 at the Harvey Potts Convention and Exposition Center on Adler Boulevard.

Our members have an expressed interest in the development, both economic and physical, of depressed inner-city neighborhoods. Your articles on the subject have earned you the admiration of many, and we would like you to address this issue as the topic of your presentation. As the expert, you are free to explore any facets of the issue that facets you wish. We will trust your judgment here.

We have general session openings on both June 27 and June 28 at 9 a.m., 10 a.m., and 2 p.m. Please let us know your preference. We are able to offer an honorarium of $1,000. Since you are a local speaker, travel expenses from your home to the convention center will not be reimbursed.

Meeting Planner Margaret Peters will be in contact with you shortly regarding your preferences and your acceptance of our offer. We certainly hope you will be able to join us. Our members are interested in your message, and who better to share that message than the expert himself?

Sincerely,

Signature

Name
Title

47c. SPEAKING ENGAGEMENTS—ACCEPTING

Date

Name/Title
Business/Organization Name
Address
City, State ZIP

Dear *(name):*

I appreciate your offer to speak at the upcoming meeting of the Association of City Councils. It is good to know that your members are aware of and appreciate my work. I will be delighted to address your group at its upcoming convention.

I prefer June 28 at 2 p.m., although I may be able to make the 10 a.m. slot as well. June 27 is our strategic planning session, and I am tied up all day. Your honorarium is graciously accepted.

I will anticipate speaking with Ms. Peters regarding further arrangements, including audiovisual needs. She can reach me at my office number Monday through Wednesday from 10:30 to 2:00.

Thank you for your interest in my work. I look forward to sharing my findings with your group.

Sincerely,

Signature

Name
Title

47d. SPEAKING ENGAGEMENTS—DECLINING

Date

Name/Title
Business/Organization Name
Address
City, State ZIP

Dear *(name):*

Many thanks for your gracious invitation to address the Association of City
Councils at its annual convention. I would gladly accept were it not for the fact that
I will be in Bombay during that month evaluating their city services.

May I suggest my colleague, Professor Jack Bruce, who has assisted me in much of
my research into urban areas. Professor Bruce specializes in the human side of
urban planning. While his focus is different from mine, we share the same basic
philosophy. I think your members will find his view equally interesting.

Professor Bruce and I share an office, and you can reach him at the same number. I
will mention that you may be calling about a speaking engagement.

Best of luck on your convention. I hope it's a successful one.

Best regards,

Signature

Name
Title

48a. Stockholders—Annual Report Letter

Date

Dear Stockholder:

Last year was a time of both challenge and change for *(name of company)*. The quantification of such an environment can be seen on the income statement. Although perhaps not as prosperous as in other years, *(name of company)* was solidly in the black in all of its divisions. It's a record of which, in these uncertain economic times, all of us may be proud.

The real value and growth is not shown in the numbers, however, but in the various reports throughout this document and in the eyes of the employees and executives who made this happen. This past year has been a time of greater productivity, operational retooling, and a general redirection of the organization. We have grown as both a business and an operational entity, and the course we have charted will guarantee continued growth and prosperity in years to come.

Your support has made this possible, and the entire board of directors thanks you for your commitment to *(name of company)*. We look forward to a continued relationship and even greater prosperity together in the future.

Sincerely,

Signature

Name
Title

48b. STOCKHOLDERS—EARNINGS ANNOUNCEMENT

Date

Dear Stockholder:

Business may be considered a chess game from time to time, with some moves marking forward motion, others a step back. As *(earnings time)* draws to an end, the Board of Directors of *(name of company)* is pleased to report positive earnings for the period.

Steady progress and a positive bottom line continue to characterize all areas of operations. Summarized earnings total *(dollar amount)*, representing a *(number)* percent *(increase/decrease)* over the last *(earnings period)*. This change can be ascribed to *(reason)*, and we have every reason to expect this trend to *(continue/change)* within the next period.

More detailed information is available for your review as a stockholder in this corporation. We appreciate your continued support and look forward to making similar reports at the close of each *(earnings period)*.

Best regards,

Signature

Name
Title

48c. Stockholders—Stock Offering Announcement

Date

Name/Title
Business/Organization Name
Address
City, State ZIP

Dear *(name):*

The Board of Directors of *(name of company)* announces that additional stock is being offered on the open market, effective *(date)*. Options will be offered to existing stockholders for fourteen days prior to the offering.

The stock is being issued to provide funds for the recent acquisition of *(name of acquired assets)* by *(name of company)*.

Contact your broker if you want to take advantage of this offer prior to its general release, or contact *(name of company)* directly at *(telephone number)* for a prospectus and purchase information.

We thank you for your past support and look forward to your continued participation in *(name of company)* and its affiliate organizations.

Sincerely,

Signature

Name
Title

49a. SUGGESTIONS—INVITING THEM FROM EMPLOYEES

MEMORANDUM

TO: Employees of the Midtown Branch
FROM: President's Office
DATE:
SUBJECT: Customer Parking

Those of you who drive to work no doubt have noticed the increasing loss of parking spaces available to customers and staff. What was once our wide-open end-of-the-mall parking lot is now full on a regular basis, thanks to the city's recently enacted Park n Ride program. Those efforts to relieve downtown congestion have increased ours.

It is not likely that the city will change its strategy, especially since the Park n Ride program has become so popular. In fact, we believe that employee and customer parking spaces will continue to decrease over time.

We have had several discussions with mall management, but to no avail. It is time for us to seek our own solutions, but, frankly, we are a little stumped. That is why we are turning to you.

We are looking for suggestions for relieving this parking congestion, and we invite you to submit your best ideas. In addition to helping relieve congestion, the employees whose recommendations are selected will also receive a gift certificate good for dinner for two at Wally's Beef Palace, along with a day off with pay.

Please submit all suggestions by September 1. Thanks for helping us with this thorny issue.

49b. Suggestions—Offering to Superiors

MEMORANDUM

TO: Vice President of Public Relations
FROM: Accounting
DATE:
SUBJECT: Client Spending

It has come to our attention that your department and you in particular spend an inordinate amount of time and money entertaining out-of-town clients. We understand that this is your job, and we appreciate your work on behalf of all of us at this company. But we note that at this rate, you will exceed your entertainment budget for the year by at least 25 percent.

We like to make a suggestion. Since much of this entertaining is done by you along with various department heads, may we suggest that those department heads be allowed to pick up a certain percentage of the tabs when discussions are germane to their business, and include it as part of their T&E expense for the project being discussed. In this way, everyone will stay within budget. It also will look less imposing to accountants and auditors than if the full amount were listed on one credit card.

We offer this a suggestion in the best interest of the company and hope you will take it as such. Thank you for your consideration.

49c. Suggestions—Offering to Peers

MEMORANDUM

TO: Vice President of Accounting
FROM: Vice President of Public Relations
DATE:
SUBJECT: Expense Suggestions

Recently I received a "suggestion" from your chief accountant as to how to better manage expenses incurred while entertaining on the company's behalf. May I "suggest" to this person that such recommendations are better received when made through the proper channels?

As department head, you are privy to discussions of budgets and procedures for managing expenses. I am sure that this person thought she was only doing her job, and that her suggestion was made respectfully. But because it did not go through you, it also was uninformed. If she were one of my staff, I would be a little miffed at her.

I know you will be able to explain to her that entertaining is budgeted under public relations so as not to put undue strain on various operational budgets and to keep them pure. I do not think her suggestion is without merit, however, and plan to bring it up during next year's budget preparation meetings. It will be up to the various department heads to decide which is the better way of handling accounting for these expenses.

But next time, tell her to check with you first. It will save all of us a little embarrassment.

49d. Suggestions—Responding Positively

MEMORANDUM

TO: Chief Teller
FROM: President's Office
DATE:
SUBJECT: Customer parking suggestion

Your suggestion for alleviating parking congestion resulting from the city's Park n Ride program was well received by the committee. More importantly, the city also considered your recommendation to move the Park n Ride lot two blocks east a good one. After some study, the city planner concluded that the new location next to the empty former auto center not only was closer and more convenient for bus drivers, but also had better access to freeway on- and off-ramps for passengers arriving to park, just as you had outlined in your suggestion.

Congratulations! There is dinner for two waiting for you at Wally's Beef Palace, as well as a day off with pay. Please coordinate the day off with your supervisor.

Thank you for your good suggestion.

49e. Suggestions—Responding Negatively

MEMORANDUM

TO: Head Loan Officer
FROM: President's Office
DATE:
SUBJECT: Customer parking suggestion

Thank you for your suggestions for relieving parking congestion resulting from the city's Park n Ride program, but we do not think filing a civil suit against the city is a good idea. The parking lot is owned by the mall from which we lease the land, and the mall is required by civic ordinance to lease a certain percentage of the lot for city improvements, a term that covers the Park n Ride program. We could sue the mall owners if our lease specified a certain percentage of the parking lot as ours. Unfortunately, it does not, giving us no legal ground whatsoever.

I appreciate your thoughts and want to encourage you to keep trying.

50a. Suppliers—Request for Bids

Date

Name/Title
Business/Organization Name
Address
City, State ZIP

Dear *(name):*

(Name of company) is about to embark on a new service initiative designed to both increase its market share and improve its position within the *(name of industry)* industry. And we are going to need your assistance to do it.

We would like to invite your bid to provide *(identification of service)* to our organization. Our new effort aims at serving *(number)* potential new customers, meaning that we will require *(measure of volume or units)* of *(name of product or service)* from your firm. We anticipate needing this service from *(start date)* to *(end date)*. All deliveries will be made to *(location and address)*.

Please respond with your best price and service scenario no later than *(date)*. Your bid will be compared to those of other companies, and the successful bidder will be notified no later than *(date)*, with those not succeeding notified shortly thereafter.

Thank you for your interest and attention. We look forward to the possibility of doing business with you.

Sincerely,

Signature

Name
Title

50b. Suppliers—Responding to Bid Invitations

Date

Name/Title
Business/Organization Name
Address
City, State ZIP

Dear *(name):*

Thank you for your recent letter of interest. We are delighted to bid on *(nature of service)* soon to be offered by your firm, and we thank you for the opportunity.

We will require no more than *(number)* days to process and ship your order for *(number)* units of *(name of product or service)* by lowest cost commercial carrier. Although we are not used to dealing in such large quantities, we are confident that we can provide a steady supply to meet your needs. Initial orders made in so large a quantity would generate a discount of *(number)* percent from the normal list price of *(dollar amount)* for a sales price of *(dollar amount)* per unit and a total price of *(dollar amount)* for the entire shipment.

Payment terms for the shipment would be *(number)* percent down prior to shipment, with the remaining payment due thirty days after delivery. Other arrangements may be made directly with our chief financial officer.

Thanks again for your interest. We look forward to a mutually rewarding relationship.

Regards,

Signature

Name
Title

50c. Suppliers—Thanking for Service

Date

Name/Title
Business/Organization Name
Address
City, State ZIP

Dear *(name):*

Business is a cutthroat game, and few relationships last more than a few months or a few years. In looking back on the service your firm has given us, however, we cannot help but smile and wonder why we have been working so well together for so long.

We found each other when this was just a three-person shop, and you were working alone. Together we grew and prospered, each able to help the other achieve his business goals. And for our part, we certainly had a good time doing so.

Thank you for all your support over the past years. As our customers know, we have become a leader in our industry. But what they do not know is that we would have had a great deal more difficulty doing so without your help and support.

Here's to an even brighter future.

Sincerely,

Signature

Name
Title

50d. Suppliers—Challenging an Order

Date

Name/Title
Business/Organization Name
Address
City, State ZIP

Dear *(name):*

We recently received shipment of *(number, name, and description of item)* listed on your bill of lading no. *(number)* and marked with our purchase order no. *(number).* Our loading dock checked in your shipment at *(time)* on *(date).*

In checking our original purchase order for that delivery, however, we note a serious discrepancy. *(Describe nature of discrepancy.)* This is not what is reflected on the purchase order, and it is not what we want or need.

The order and paperwork have been set aside pending further explanation. Please contact *(name)* in our shipping office and he will attempt to work through this discrepancy with you. He also will set a time for you to pick up the mistakenly shipped merchandise and deliver what we actually need.

We appreciate your timely attention to this matter. We have customers who will be needing this material soon, and we would hate to have to tell them it is not here as a result of manufacturer error.

Sincerely,

Signature

Name
Title

50e. Suppliers—Responding to Order Challenge

Date

Name/Title
Business/Organization Name
Address
City, State ZIP

Dear *(name):*

Your recent letter caused us concern, so we went back and carefully reviewed your original purchase order no. *(number)* and our shipping bill no. *(number),* dated *(date).*

Your hunch was correct. We did have a major snafu here at the warehouse. Your order was intermingled with another order on our loading dock, and some of the boxes were mislabeled. The other customer also called to complain, and quick cross-referencing between the two purchase orders and the two delivery bills confirmed our suspicions.

Please accept our apology. A special shipment has been dispatched, and by now you should have received the correct merchandise and had that which you did not order picked up. If this has not happened, please call me personally, and I will immediately rectify the situation myself.

We hope this mix-up has not caused either you or your customers any undue inconvenience. If there is anything further we can do, please do not hesitate to call.

Thank you for the opportunities both to serve you and to rectify our mistake.

Sincerely,

Signature

Name
Title

50f. Suppliers—Challenging a Price

Date

Name/Title
Business/Organization Name
Address
City, State ZIP

Dear *(name)*:

Thank you for your prompt shipment of *(name and/or nature of goods)*. We always know that we can expect immediate and excellent service when dealing with your firm.

In reviewing our invoice, however, we note a discrepancy between our understanding of the price and that listed on the invoice. Your bill shows a price of *(total amount)*, or *(dollar amount)* per unit. Our original order stipulated a total cost of *(dollar amount)*, or *(dollar amount)* per unit. The billed price would force us to either price the merchandise above our customers' range or reduce our profit margin.

We are holding your bill until a satisfactory explanation and corrected invoice are forthcoming. We are sure this is merely the result of some accounting oversight, and we will pay the correct amount as soon as the invoice arrives.

We appreciate your timely response in this matter.

Sincerely,

Signature

Name
Title

50g. Suppliers—Responding to Price Challenge

Date

Name/Title
Business/Organization Name
Address
City, State ZIP

Dear *(name)*:

Your recent letter prompted a close review of the written order no. *(number)* and a discussion with *(name)*, who sold you the merchandise. We appreciate your concern, but all our evidence shows that the price billed was the price quoted. The price you claim we offered does not cover manufacturing modifications to meet your specifications.

Clearly, we have a miscommunication here, one that we would like to resolve in an amicable fashion. Your business is very important to us, yet we cannot afford the price you say you have been quoted. Perhaps there is a middle ground where we both can be happy.

May I take the liberty of scheduling lunch for us *(day, date)* at *(location)* to discuss this? Our history goes back some way in an industry not known for long-term alliances. I would like to maintain that relationship if possible.

Thank you for your understanding in this matter. My secretary will call you to confirm *(day)*'s luncheon.

Sincerely,

Signature

Name
Title

50h. Suppliers—Confirming an Order

Date

Name/Title
Business/Organization Name
Address
City, State ZIP

Dear *(name):*

Thank you for your recent telephone order of *(date)*. This letter serves to confirm that order in writing.

Specifically, you ordered *(name, nature and number of merchandise)* to be delivered on *(date)* by lowest-cost commercial carrier to *(name, address)*. The invoice will be sent to *(name, address)* concurrent with delivery.

If this is not the order you placed, please contact us immediately and we will rectify the order prior to shipping. If an incomplete or incorrect order arrives, please contact us.

Thanks again for purchasing from us. We appreciate your business.

Sincerely,

Signature

Name
Title

50i. Suppliers—Complaint

Date

Name/Title
Business/Organization Name
Address
City, State ZIP

Dear *(name):*

For the last *(number)* years, we have enjoyed dealing with your firm. The quality of merchandise has been high, and the service courteous and prompt. Frankly, we have had no complaints. Until now.

(Outline nature and detail of complaint.)

We would appreciate a swift resolution of this matter. To date we have enjoyed our ongoing working relationship. If this situation is not rectified, however, that relationship may have to end.

Thank you for your understanding and assistance in this matter.

Sincerely,

Signature

Name
Title

50j. SUPPLIERS—RESPONDING TO A COMPLAINT

Date

Name/Title
Business/Organization Name
Address
City, State ZIP

Dear *(name)*:

We were dismayed by your recent letter regarding *(nature of the problem)*. Rest assured that we have dealt with the matter, and please accept our sincere apologies for any inconvenience this may have caused.

*(**Optional paragraph**: Outline the problem and its resolution.)*

Thank you for bringing this to our attention. We appreciate the opportunity to correct this matter and hope we will be able to continue doing business together.

Again, please accept our apologies.

Regards,

Signature

Name
Title

51a. THANK YOU—FOR THE CONTRIBUTION

Date

Name/Title
Business/Organization Name
Address
City, State ZIP

Dear *(name):*

The board of directors of the Toledo Theater Guild would like to thank you for the kindness of your recent donation.

This fall promises to be a busy season for the guild, with four dramatic productions and two musical revues. Ticket receipts and corporate donations support only so much of our effort. It is private donations like yours that make it possible for the show to go on, and we could not do it without you.

As a special recognition, we are holding a Contributors Night: a pre-opening performance of Tennessee Williams' *A Streetcar Named Desire*, with M*A*S*H's Jamie Farr as Stanley Kowalski and Sandy Duncan as the immortal Blanche DuBois. I think it will be a night long remembered among those involved in Toledo's theater world.

We look forward to having you join us for a special evening for special people.

With thanks and appretiation,

Signature

Name
Title

51b. THANK YOU—FOR THE SUPPORT

Date

Name/Title
Business/Organization Name
Address
City, State ZIP

Dear *(name):*

Civic improvement is never easy, and the influx of external interest groups makes it just that much harder. If it were not for people like you, good referenda would never pass. To that end, the Mayor's Office of the City of Savannah would like to extend its heartiest thanks.

Influential business leaders wield a tremendous amount of influence, even in such a parochial town as ours. For you to come out so forthrightly in favor of the current initiatives sent a strong signal to voters who otherwise might have vacillated on the issues. It also sent a bright shining flare up in my camp. It is nice to know who my friends are.

Thanks again for your support. If I can ever return the favor, please feel free to ask.

Sincerely,

Signature

Name
Title

51c. THANK YOU—FOR THE PROMOTION

Date

Name/Title
Business/Organization Name
Address
City, State ZIP

Dear *(name):*

Thank you for the promotion and for the faith it exhibits in my ability to get things done. We all like to think we are head-turners and world-beaters, but few of us have the chance to prove it. You have given me that chance, and I am very grateful.

I guarantee you will not be disappointed.

Sincerely,

Signature

Name
Title

51d. THANK YOU—FOR THE INTERVIEW

Date

Name/Title
Business/Organization Name
Address
City, State ZIP

Dear (name):

Many thanks for taking the time to meet with me today and explain the exciting opportunities available through your organization. Businesses survive only if they have the strength, will, and ability to do so. Based on the senior leadership team members I met during our day together, it is easy to see why your company is ahead of the rest.

I came away with a new enthusiasm for both our business and your firm. I am interested and honored that you have chosen me to interview. Now I only hope I have the opportunity to prove to you I am capable of running with the best.

Sincerely,

Signature

Name
Title

51e. THANK YOU—FOR THE BONUS/RAISE

Date

Name/Title
Business/Organization Name
Address
City, State ZIP

Dear *(name):*

Just a short note to thank you very much for the generous *(bonus/raise)* you gave me during this past pay period. I have tried my best to help further the interests of this organization, and I can tell by this sharing of the wealth that I have at least made a small contribution.

More important than the money, however, is the appreciation for and faith in my abilities that it represents. In today's world, our self-confidence is challenged in so many ways that it is especially meaningful when our efforts are so generously recognized and rewarded.

Sincerely,

Signature

Name
Title

51f. THANK YOU—FOR THE HOSPITALITY

Date

Name/Title
Business/Organization Name
Address
City, State ZIP

Dear *(name):*

This is just a short note to thank you for your gracious hospitality during my recent business trip to your city. You went out of your way in taking me as a guest in your home, and the dinner you served was wonderful.

I am pleased we were able to conclude our agreement to work together and that we also had a chance to strengthen our personal relationship. I look forward to seeing our project develop and to our next meeting.

Thanks again,

With warm regards,

Signature

Name
Title

51g. THANK YOU—FOR THE REFERENCE/REFERRAL

Date

Name/Title
Business/Organization Name
Address
City, State ZIP

Dear *(name):*

When it came time to choose, they said there were several of us with excellent qualifications, but only one with the type of references they sought. I was that person, and I am now more than gainfully employed thanks to your kind words and cooperation.

After our past working relationship, I was not sure what type of reference you might have been willing to give. I was very flattered when I read it, and the interviewer was impressed. I had some doubts about the quality of my credentials. But I had no doubts about the quality of your reference. It was like gold.

Thanks again for your generous assistance.

Best regards,

Signature

Name
Title

51h. THANK YOU—FOR THE VOTE

Date

Name/Title
Business/Organization Name
Address
City, State ZIP

Dear *(name):*

When all is said and done, it will not matter who won or lost any election. What will matter is the loyalty and support of those who showed the strength and fortitude to stand by an unpopular candidate in the face of overwhelming odds because they believed what that person had to say. That's where you come in.

Thank you for your unflagging support. It means as much to me as being elected. The best part is that I look forward to working with you in the future on the many issues on which we share a common concern and approach.

Best regards,

Signature

Name
Title

52a. Transmittals—Documents

Date

Name/Title
Business/Organization Name
Address
City, State ZIP

Dear *(name):*

Here are the technical specifications for the System XP6 you requested. They should aid in answering the questions you had about downloading data to personal computers.

In addition to the operations manual, we have enclosed schematics of the circuitry and other technical documentation that will help you better understand the system and its functions. A toll-free troubleshooting number is also enclosed. When asked for your system ID number, say you are a factory representative working in the Westchester office.

If you need any more information, please call. Satisfying customers is our most important goal.

With best regards,

Signature

Name
Title

52b. Transmittals—Staff

Date

Name/Title
Business/Organization Name
Address
City, State ZIP

Dear *(name):*

These orders accompany the transfer of members of the 34th Armored Division to your command. The twenty-eight soldiers represent what is left of what once was a full armored command. They are to be merged into your forces and reassigned to new divisions.

Direct any questions to your battalion commander.

Cordially,

Signature

Name
Title

53a. Use of Name or Title—Requesting

Date

Name/Title
Business/Organization Name
Address
City, State ZIP

Dear *(name):*

Our good name and status is something each of us jealously guards, for it is something earned only through hard work and public recognition. Yet when we have the opportunity to share the benefit that name may have with a worthy cause, many of us give willingly in the hopes that our support will lend assistance to those less fortunate than ourselves.

There are few members of the Dearborn, Michigan, community who don't recognize the *(last name)* name or the influence the family has had in building a safe place for our families and children to live, learn, and work. But the economy has taken its toll on even a community as prosperous as Dearborn, and a growing number of families are finding themselves without adequate food, clothing, or shelter.

The *(name of company/foundation)*'s mission is to help such people, but it needs continued corporate funding in order to do its work. The association of your name with the foundation will open many doors in the community. Your involvement with our campaign will show by example the importance of our foundation's work.

Our fall campaign will be coming up in sixty days, and we'd like to include your name on the roster of our supporters. We've also taken the liberty of preparing a fundraising letter that includes your name as one of our sponsors to be sent to residents of the *(residential area)* and *(residential area)* neighborhoods. With your approval, we will mail this appeal to the county's 1,000 most affluent households in hopes of raising a half-million dollars. That effort alone will fund our work for the first half of the new year. All it takes is your agreement on the use of your name.

May we count you in as a supporter in name of the *(name of company/foundation)*? Your contribution would mean more to us than you'll ever know.

Sincerely,

Signature

Name
Title

53b. Use of Name or Title—Seeking More Information

Date

Name/Title
Business/Organization Name
Address
City, State ZIP

Dear *(name)*:

I received your letter asking for permission to use my name in your upcoming fundraising efforts. I also have thoroughly familiarized myself with the *(name of company/foundation)*. Of all the charities that seek my assistance or support, few have worked as hard with as little or have done as much as your organization. I am impressed with your past successes.

Before I give you approval to use my name, however, I need to know more about the focus of this campaign and how and to whom its funds will be disbursed. I also would like to see and have my attorney review the letter as well as establish limits and guidelines on how the letter may be used.

In years past, I've known executives like me who have lent their names to sloppy and/or unscrupulous charities and have wound up facing lawsuits as a result. I have every wish to assist your efforts, but I think both our needs will be best served if we establish some boundaries.

Feel free to contact my assistant, *(name)*, to set up an appointment. I look forward to meeting with you and discovering how I can assist the *(name of company/foundation)*.

Best regards,

Signature

Name
Title

53c. USE OF NAME OR TITLE—GRANTING PERMISSION

Date

Name/Title
Business/Organization Name
Address
City, State ZIP

Dear *(name)*:

Thank you for taking the time to visit with me last Thursday about using my name in your upcoming fundraising campaign to help the homeless. My previous research had prepared me for what I had hoped would be a noble effort. But your business plan for fundraising and disbursement significantly exceeded my expectations. I came away from our meeting very impressed with your goals and methodologies.

Feel free to use my name and title on your fundraising letter to the *(residential area)* and *(residential area)* townships, as well as any attendant publicity associated with either the campaign or the *(name of foundation)*. I have every confidence that you'll not only reach but exceed your goal, and I'm proud to contribute whatever I can to the cause.

Sincerely,

Signature

Name
Title

53d. Use of Name or Title—Refusing Permission

Date

Name/Title
Business/Organization Name
Address
City, State ZIP

Dear *(name):*

Thank you for meeting with me regarding my assistance in your upcoming fundraising effort. However, after a review of your policies, procedures, and initiatives, I'm afraid I will have to deny you usage of my name and title.

In the past, Dearborn and its surrounding communities have been the target of some poorly planned and executed fundraising efforts. Those who innocently lent their names to such efforts, while not suffering legal consequences, have paid a price in terms of status and opportunity.

While your heart may be in the right place, numerous elements of your effort bear resemblance to some of these past misguided efforts. Contributors who have been burned before will recognize these immediately and pass their own judgement on those involved. I cannot be connected to that sort of thing.

I'm sorry I couldn't be of more service.

Regards,

Signature

Name
Title

53e. USE OF NAME OR TITLE—THANK YOU

Date

Name/Title
Business/Organization Name
Address
City, State ZIP

Dear *(name):*

We're still counting the pledges in support of Dearborn's homeless, but we're thrilled to report that they already have reached more than $225,000. And contributions are still coming in!

Central to those fundraising efforts were monies generated in the *(residential area)* and *(residential area)* townships from among recipients receiving the letter on which you were a sponsor. I don't know if you have the power to make it rain or turn wine to water, but it seems that everything your name touches turns to gold on behalf of the needy. We couldn't be more pleased.

The staff and volunteers of the *(name of company/foundation)* and the homeless of Dearborn thank you from the bottom of their hearts for your kind assistance. We might have been able to do it without you, but we certainly wouldn't have wanted to try.

Sincerely,

Signature

Name
Title

54a. Welcome—New Employee

Date

Name/Title
Business/Organization Name
Address
City, State ZIP

Dear *(name):*

By now you have had your orientation lecture, met with your supervisor, perhaps even had lunch with your peers. Certainly you have settled into your office if you are reading this. After all that, let me take this opportunity to welcome you to *(name of company).*

We have a proud heritage of service to the *(name of industry)* industry, and we welcome bright people who are willing to help us improve that service. You have passed through several layers of scrutiny to get where you are, and we are excited to have you on board. I personally look forward to working with you.

If you have any specific questions, contact either your supervisor or HR. If I can be of any assistance in helping you get settled or answer any questions about our organization's higher mission, please feel free to call on me.

Thanks for joining us. Good luck in your new position.

Sincerely,

Signature

Name
Title

54b. WELCOME—NEW CLIENT

Date

Name/Title
Business/Organization Name
Address
City, State ZIP

Dear *(name):*

We pride ourselves on personalized service and going the extra mile. To that end, we would like to welcome you as the newest client of *(name of company).*

Our goal is personalized service, and our regional sales representative should be calling on you shortly. He will ask you to complete a personal service profile like the one enclosed for us to keep on file. It answers frequently asked questions and provides information for our database.

Please note the telephone number on this letterhead. Though it is very unlikely, if ever you feel you are not getting the service you deserve, feel free to call that number. Think of it as a hot line to the executive suite. We will go out of our way to make sure you are satisfied.

Sincerely,

Signature

Name
Title

54c. WELCOME—NEW SUPPLIER

Date

Name/Title
Business/Organization Name
Address
City, State ZIP

Dear *(name):*

With the signing of the enclosed contract, we would like to welcome you as a supplier to our company. We have a high demand for quality and no tolerance for error. Based on our research, that also describes your firm. We are glad to be doing business with you.

(Name) will be your primary contact for all incoming materials and orders. If you have a question about payment, contact *(name)* in our accounting office. *(He/she)* will help you sort the matter out.

Again, welcome aboard. If there is anything we can do to help facilitate this new relationship, please do not hesitate to ask.

Sincerely,

Signature

Name
Title

54d. WELCOME—NEW SHAREHOLDER

Date

Name/Title
Business/Organization Name
Address
City, State ZIP

Dear *(name):*

Welcome to the ranks of ownership of *(name of corporation).* As a new shareholder, you are entitled to all the rights and privileges of ownership, including full financial disclosure. To that end, we have enclosed our most recent financial statements.

The annual shareholders' meeting is held the first week of June at the end of our fiscal year. You have a right to attend and vote on issues important to your ownership, or you may appoint a proxy to act on your behalf. Meeting and voting materials will be mailed to you approximately one month prior to the annual meeting.

If you have any questions you may contact either the chairman of the board or myself. Welcome again to the ranks of ownership.

Sincerely,

Signature

Name
Title

54e. WELCOME—NEW BOARD MEMBER

Date

Name/Title
Business/Organization Name
Address
City, State ZIP

Dear *(name):*

Welcome to the board of directors of *(name of company).* We were delighted when you announced your candidacy. We are even more pleased now that you are able to take your place at the company's boardroom table.

Your new board member orientation packet is enclosed with this letter. Please read through it thoroughly before next month's meeting. It describes the rights and privileges of your position, as well as the obligations associated with service. Serving on a board is no longer an honorary position. You will want to be well versed in your obligations so that you can perform them fully.

If you have any questions, please contact the chairman or myself. Otherwise, let the record show that we enthusiastically welcome you to the board of directors.

Sincerely,

Signature

Name
Title

Focus on E-Mail

E-Mail and Its Uses

One great advantage of the growing computer Internet is not instant access to mountains of information—although that, too, has appeal—but rather the communication interactivity available through electronic mail. Everyone from rocker David Bowie to President Bill Clinton logs on to the 'net to swap dialogue and ideas with invisible users all linked by telephone lines.

Offices, businesses, and industries are making increasing use of e-mail networks to communicate with remote offices, talk with salespeople on the road, and even hold dialogues with suppliers and competitors on issues of mutual interest.

Whether it is through nationwide commercial services such as Prodigy or America Online, local area networks (called LANs) within departments or companies, or some variation in between, everyone is logging on to e-mail.

E-Mail by Application

Why use e-mail when you can just pick up the telephone? Because e-mail messages, while immediate, also are permanent, can be printed out to become part of the record, and can be broadcast to numerous recipients. Why, then, not simply write letters? Because e-mail's immediacy allows the receiver the choice of either responding instantly or, if the subject is especially sensitive, thinking about the message, maybe sharing the idea with others, and formulating a careful response.

This electronic hybrid is really the best of both communication alternatives, and one that has become increasingly popular with business users. In fact, e-mail has replaced some meetings, shortening unnecessary discussions and producing more immediate results. Used well, e-mail can be a very effective communication shorthand.

Unfortunately, it has also tended to replace human interactivity in some offices. That may increase efficiency, but employee relations can be damaged when all communications take place over the network. And people who are proficient at writing tend to wield more influence than those who struggle with sentence structure. In fact, those who communicate poorly in writing may actually suffer from excessive e-mail usage because their full capabilities are masked by their grammatical weaknesses.

But in the end, e-mail is simply one more office tool—albeit an influential one—that can help increase communication efficiency and effectiveness when kept in the proper perspective.

WHEN IS E-MAIL MOST EFFECTIVE?

Different users see different values in intraoffice e-mail, but the technology is most effective when the content is limited to:

- Updates to issues affecting a multitude of users, such as whole departments.
- Questions either answered or asked on behalf of departments, organizations, or individuals within them.
- Clarifications of issues, procedures, or other policy questions that entire groups need to know.
- Conversations, either business-related or frivolous, that bond the users together. That, in fact, is the secret to any network's success for most users.
- Reports, generally the shorter the better, to one or a group of people.
- Data transfer, generally through attached files holding longer documents, between cooperating staff or departments.

A FEW E-MAIL CAUTIONS

E-mail's transmission and delivery advantages already have been discussed. Those also form the basis for several e-mail cautions.

- Unlike telephone calls, e-mail messages have permanence. Including information or language that is confidential, indiscreet, or otherwise sensitive given the nature of the business environment is always dangerous. A former instructor once said that nothing should ever be put in writing that you would not want to see plastered across page one of *The New York Times*. That is a little extreme, perhaps, but you get the idea.

- Often e-mail messages are broadcast to a network of recipients. Most recipients respect the nature and intent of the message. However, most e-mail systems also allow recipients to forward messages to users for whom they were not originally intended. In the interest of good communication, many well-meaning e-mailers have forwarded a message whose content and/or tone irritated or embarrassed second-party readers. Maybe our former instructor's caution was not so extreme after all.

- Finally, e-mail messages also tend to hang around long after their content has been digested. Sensitive or inappropriate transmissions should be deleted as soon as possible from all recipient and sender files in which they appear. Most systems have a mechanism by which senders can see not only if their messages have been received, but also if they have been read. Be careful with what you share, lest you find it innocently transmitted to someone who should not be in that particular information loop. When in doubt, remember to apply *The New York Times* rule.

Ironically, the best overall advice about e-mail comes from William Shakespeare, who said "Brevity is the soul of wit." Keep your e-mails short, conversational, and sweet and they will generate a much better response.

Following are several examples of effective e-mail:

1A. ANNOUNCEMENTS

The human resources department, with the company president's approval, announces that a new holiday will be added to the seven current holidays on next year's calendar. In addition to New Year's Day, Martin Luther King Jr. Day, Memorial Day, Independence Day, Labor Day, Thanksgiving Day, and Christmas Day, the company also will be closed on Christmas Eve Day so that employees can make holiday preparations with their families. Please be prepared to enjoy that day to the fullest.

1B. ANNOUNCEMENTS

Break out the cigars and balloons. Susan finally had her baby last night at Baxter Memorial Hospital! It was an 8-pound 6-ounce, 19-inch baby girl, Jeanne Marie, and both mother and daughter are reportedly doing fine. The department will send a flowering plant, but anyone wishing to send an individual card or gift may do so after tomorrow to Susan's home address as listed on the employee roster.

2. CLARIFICATION OF FACT/RUMOR

Word has reached the fourth floor that some employees fear that because of economic hard times and service cutbacks, their jobs may be eliminated and they may become unemployed right before Christmas. Figures range from 10 percent to 35 percent of all staff, depending on which rumor you hear.

While these are, indeed, hard times for our industry, management has no plans to cut staff before the end of the year, or even during the first quarter of next year. Cost containment measures to offset our financial downturn currently are underway, and have been for some time. But rest assured that they don't include any staff cuts whatsoever.

If you are still concerned about the security of your job or this organization, please talk to your supervisor or the director of human resources. We value all our employees and the work they do. Eliminating their services would be our very last resort.

3A. CONFIDENTIAL QUERIES/INFORMATION—ASKING

We've talked several times about possible avenues for promotion in an organization that, while it's a great place to work, really offers little for aggressive employees beyond a certain level. The combination of employee shifts and new work brought into the department recently indicate that there might be such an opportunity. And right now that information may be crucial to my future decisions.

Can I look forward to a promotion soon? Another firm is currently interested in me and may be on the verge of making an offer. My loyalty is here, but I can't afford to pass this up if there's just nowhere else to go.

3B. CONFIDENTIAL QUERIES/INFORMATION—ANSWERING

This is a subject best not discussed via e-mail, but as long as you asked, I will gladly answer. Yes, there will be opportunities for movement to management-level positions within this department in the next six months. Yes, your work record has been good, and your skills are such that you may be considered for one of these positions. But as for making promises at this point, I can't in good conscience advise you to pass up opportunities that interest you. The management team has yet to make a decision, and until they do, all options are open.

We would hate to lose you, but we also can't advise you to give up any and all other opportunities. You have to follow your own good judgment. Whatever that is, we wish you the best.

4. CONVERSATION

Q: John and Bob are thinking of a fishing trip to the mountains the weekend of the 28th and 29th. Nothing fancy. A little R&R, some trolling, and a chance to eat trout and drink beer for breakfast without having to shave. Are you up for something like that?
A: Dunno. I think I may have a wedding to go to that weekend. I jumped ship on the last one, and if I don't make this one, I don't think my in-laws will ever forgive me. Not to mention my wife. When do you need to know by?

Q: We're looking for a fourth, and Bob and I would prefer you. But if you can't make it, we'll have to take (shudder) Jimmy because he's a good friend of John's. Why don't you check with Peggy and let us know by next Monday? Meanwhile I'll try to think of someone other than (shudder) Jimmy in case you're wedding-bound.
A: Peg says the wedding's off. It seems the bride (her niece) got cold feet once again and backed out at the last minute. Guess we'll just put the gift in the closet for another year. I'm already tying my flies, so count me in and plan on leaving (shudder) Jimmy at home.

5. LEAVE REQUEST

I would like to take the Friday before and the Tuesday after Labor Day as personal holidays. Since it's the end of the summer, the five-day weekend will give Mary and me a chance to go up to the cottage and bring in the boat dock.

Thanks for your consideration.

6. MEETING ANNOUNCEMENT

The senior management team will convene Friday morning at 8 a.m. in the Hart Conference Room to discuss next year's budget. Please be prepared with your rough operating estimates. We're going to have to take a hard look at staff training, travel, and capital purchases again this year. Plan to justify any expenditure requests in this area by showing concrete value to the organization in terms of cost savings, improved efficiencies, or increased revenue.

We'll begin promptly at 8:00. Rolls and coffee will be served.

7. MEETING MINUTES

Yesterday's staff meeting, while abbreviated, produced several good ideas ready for immediate implementation. Detailed minutes will follow in hard copy, but an operational recap and duty roster are in order here so that we may proceed.

- Jack Jeffers agreed that manufacturing could do without one-third of its storage and operating space and will immediately begin clearing that area to ease the overflow problems currently being felt by shipping. Jack estimated that it would take four to six days before shipping could begin moving in.

- Public Relations will conduct an employee satisfaction survey within the next two to four weeks to probe for soft spots in morale and determine where better training may be needed. Martha Bright said she would have reliable data to share within six weeks. All managers will participate in decisions made based on these findings.

- Sales and Marketing has assembled a crack team of specialists to invade the Cincinnati market. Amy Wong will head the squad in search of potential markets for our products throughout the Ohio River Valley.

The next meeting of the team is scheduled for Friday the 31st. Plan on updating your individual section efforts to manage costs.

8. OPEN DIALOGUE

Q: My computer seems to be acting up. Anyone out there have any problems transferring from the e-mail program into the edit program in order to print?

A1: I've also had a few problems, especially in trying to block and move documents once I've made the transfer. If you find an answer, let me know.

A2: Neither of you needs to transfer to the edit program if all you want to do is print. Hit Shift/1 and you'll see Print Menu options. The full document is A, a single page is B. To review print parameters, hit C.

A1: That doesn't work for me because of the way my disk is formatted. Other people have given me that advice, and it hasn't helped. I think I'm going to need a more creative solution.

Q: Well, I just tried it and it works for me. Thanks for the tip! Any more good advice you can share?

9. PERSONAL ISSUES/TOPICS

I'm going to need a few days off this next week. My father is in the hospital, and they don't think he's going to make it. I hate to even think of this, but it looks like I may have a funeral to plan. I've made sure all my projects are covered and deadlines met, and I think the department will run smoothly while I'm gone. I'd also appreciate some flexibility in case this takes longer or is more painful than I think it will be.

10. POLICY ANNOUNCEMENT

Effective September 1, this company will be considered a smoke-free workplace and no more tobacco product consumption will be allowed on company premises. This also includes the first and third floor break rooms, which had come to be considered smoking rooms. These, too, will be smoke-free environments.

The measure, adopted as Policy No. 88-474, isn't designed to penalize employees who smoke, but to make the workplace safer for those who don't. We also encourage current smokers to quit, and the company will be happy to fund attendance at any authorized stop smoking clinic or workshop for any employee and his or her immediate family members who smoke.

This measure has been taken in accordance with civic ordinance and for the better health of us all.

11. PROCEDURES

In the event of a fire alarm, employees are directed to do the following:

- Proceed immediately to the nearest stairwell in a swift but orderly fashion, refraining from excessive noise. DO NOT USE THE ELEVATORS. Electric power will probably be turned off, and you will be trapped inside.

- Do not attempt to save any personal or company belongings. Employee safety is our first and foremost concern.

- Upon leaving the building, walk through the parking lot and move away from the structure. Allow firefighters ample room to work.

- Do not attempt to make telephone calls prior to leaving. Any calls you may be involved in must be ended immediately upon the sound of the alarm.

- All supervisors have been deputized as fire marshals. Look to them for further guidance and answers to any questions.

Observation of these procedures will mean greater safety for us all. In the event of emergency, please adhere strictly to these guidelines.

12. PUBLIC RECOGNITION

You may read about it in the company newsletter, but let us be the first to announce that Ray Lopez has been promoted to senior partner of this firm. Ray, who has been with us for five years, has made excellent contributions to both the reputation and the financial well-being of our company. In addition, his skills have attracted significant new business, including three of our ten largest clients. This promotion recognizes those contributions and the value of these contributions to the well-being of us all.

A formal reception will be held in the Board Room Friday from 2 to 4 p.m. We hope you all will attend. And please remember to congratulate Ray for a job well done when you see him in the hallway. He deserves it.

13. REMINDERS

Just a reminder that the company Picnic and Softball Extravaganza is scheduled for Saturday, August 6, in Lodz Park. There will be a playground and games for the kids, along with door prizes and contests for the adults. Hot dogs, burgers, soft drinks, and beer will be served, along with buckets of Mrs. Coulee's famous potato salad.

Come early, stay late, eat much and often. It's a good chance to renew old friendships and make new ones.

14. REQUESTS

Would all employees please remember to shut off their office lights and close their doors prior to departing for the evening? The cleaning crew will not clean any office it thinks may be occupied, and offices with lights still on are good candidates for occupation. If your office hasn't been cleaned in a while . . . well, now you know why.

15. RESPONSES

I got your e-mail about meeting this Saturday morning. While it will take a little shuffling on my part, plan to see me at 8:00 as requested. You've been more than fair with your liberal leave policies, and I think it's the least we can do to make the most of opportunities during this crisis.

Would you like me to bring anything? Coffee? Rolls? Aspirin?

16. SALES UPDATE

The following are sales figures for various markets for the last quarter. These are highlights from the complete reports you will receive at the end of the month.

NORTHEAST	
Sales Revenue	$164,897
Operating Expense	$123,105
Net Income	$41,792
SOUTHEAST	
Sales Revenue	$417,567
Operating Expense	$200,098
Net Income	$217,069
MIDWEST	
Sales Revenue	$350,554
Operating Expense	$186,112
Net Income	$164,442
WEST	
Sales Revenue	$499,706
Operating Revenue	$375,111
Net Income	$124,595

Direct all questions to the national sales manager.